The Magnificent Cuckold

For Richard and David,

with love,

2006

Fernand Crommelynck

THE MAGNIFICENT CUCKOLD

(Le Cocu Magnifique)

A Farce in Three Acts

Translated by Ben Sonnenberg & Amiel Melnick

With illustrations by Robert Andrew Parker

GRAND STREET BOOKS

NEW YORK

To my dear René Delange, fraternally
—F.C.

Design by Deborah Thomas.
Translation copyright © 2006 by Ben Sonnenberg and Amiel Melnick.

Illustrations © by Robert Andrew Parker.

ISBN: 1-931824-20-7
Library of Congress: 2006926263

The translators gratefully acknowledge the help and encouragement
of Richard Howard.

Le Cocu Magnifique was first produced in Paris on December 18th, 1920,
at the Théâtre de L'Œuvre.

Grand Street Books are published by the Grand Street Foundation, Inc.
at 50 Riverside Drive, New York, NY 10024.

CHARACTERS

STELLA
CORNELIA
FLORENCE, *Cornelia's sister*
ROMANIE, *Stella's old nurse*
THE HERDSMAN
THE COUNT
BRUNO
ESTRUGO
THE MAYOR
PETRUS
THE BOY FROM OOSTKERQUE

The action takes place in Flanders in the early 1920s.

ACT ONE

(The interior of an old watermill that has been converted to a residence. Vast living room with high, white walls, lit mostly by two windows at back; one on the ground floor and the other higher up.

The first window looks out on a garden full of flowers that stretches to the edge of the road. The second window, at the top of a wooden staircase, opens onto a wide blue sky. An interior balcony, reached by the staircase, leads to the bedrooms at right.

The outside door is at left, towards the back; the door to the rooms at right, downstage.

All the woodwork, doors, window frames, staircase and balcony, are painted a pleasant, rustic green, somewhat milky in tone. The furniture—armoires, tables, stands and wooden chairs—are painted straw yellow and varnished.

STELLA kneels on the floor near the window, in front of a canary cage and pots of geraniums.)

STELLA *(addressing a plant)*: You want more? More? What would you do if I wasn't here? You'd wait for rain until you died, you'd dry up in the noonday sun. *(To the canary)* And you, little thing, you're thirsty too? What would *you* do if I wasn't here? Would you sing? Not without your birdseed you wouldn't, without your bits of lettuce, your wet lumps of sugar. That's right, flap your wings. You'd fly away into the forest? *(She laughs.)* You don't even know the right things to eat. You wouldn't last a day!

You were born to live in a cage, and you were born to live in a pot, and me—lucky girl—I was born to love my Bruno! *(She laughs.)* Is that what the Good Lord intended?

You, you have your flowers; you have your song; and me—lucky girl—I have Bruno! What if you were free in a garden, what if you were free in a tree and what if I were without my love, who would guide us? (Yes, tweet tweet!)… There's nothing: just thunder.

(She waters the plants, feeds the bird.)

What were you dreaming about, you in your yellow feathers? Plants dream too, sometimes, on starry nights. No, it must be at dawn.

As for me, I've forgotten my dream.

(Pretending to be childishly sad) When Bruno gets back, I won't have anything to tell him. Oh!… I slept alone, on sheets, in the middle of the bed, and I've forgotten my dream! What will my beloved say?

(CORNELIA, a young woman from the village, passing by on the road, pauses at the window.)

CORNELIA: Hello, Stella, I saw your man this morning.

STELLA *(leaping up at once)*: What? You saw him? I'm so happy! Oh, and so sad! Where did you see him?

CORNELIA: At the North Gate.

STELLA: This morning?

CORNELIA: Just as it was getting light. I was coming back in the cart with my sister.

STELLA *(moved)*: And you saw him? (Good morning, Cornelia.) And you saw him? Was he happy? Did he say anything about me? *(She calls out.)* Nana! Nana! —Well?

CORNELIA: I stopped the horse. He came over and leaned against the shaft.

STELLA *(calls again)*: Nana! Nana!

CORNELIA: He'd been walking for ages and he was hot. He took off his cap…

STELLA *(animated)*: Wait a minute!

(ROMANIE, the old nurse, appears at right. STELLA goes to her.)

Nana, here's someone who saw Bruno, this morning, at the North Gate. Isn't that right, Cornelia? She saw him, saw (where's your sister?), saw Bruno! He came up and leaned against the shaft of the wagon, he was hot, he took off his cap. You tell it, Cornelia! And then?

CORNELIA: He went his way and we went ours.

STELLA: But before that, what did he say?

CORNELIA: Something about the weather, I think...

STELLA: Is that all?

CORNELIA: I don't remember...

STELLA (*hiding in her nurse's arms, she abruptly bursts into tears.*): Oh! Nurse! Nurse! She doesn't remember my sweet Bruno's words. How could she not?

THE NURSE (*consoling her*): There, there! Calm yourself.... You want me to cry too? Bruno's on his way, little slave, we'll get our Bruno back.

STELLA: But we have to wait three whole hours!

THE NURSE: Calm yourself ... He'll be so loving... Don't be jealous! He'll tell us about his long journey, about what happened on the way, and about which trees are blooming and what people hope for in the towns and all, and about how he thought he was losing us every step of the way, and more...

CORNELIA (*outside, bursting out laughing*): Holy mother of God! The man's eaten out their brains!

STELLA: Cornelia, let me kiss you! (*CORNELIA lets herself be kissed.*) Now call your sister. Maybe she'll have more to tell us?

CORNELIA (*calls*): Florence! Hey! Flo!

STELLA (*impatient*): Is she coming? Bruno's been gone since last night. He's bringing my cousin back with him. He's captain of a ship!

CORNELIA: Hey! Florence! Come here!

STELLA: Do you remember my cousin Petrus? Is she coming? (*FLORENCE appears at the window, out of breath.*)

FLORENCE: Come home right now, Cornelia! The brewer's men are here.

STELLA: Florence, you saw Bruno on the road. Please tell me, did he say anything about me?

FLORENCE *(laughs)*: Oh, yes, he was holding a flower in his mouth. *(She takes a flower out of the pocket of her apron and throws it to STELLA.)* Catch, it's from him to you. *(She runs off with her sister.)* Hurry up, lazy, we have work to do!

THE NURSE: You see, Stella dear, he sent you a primrose, the first of the season! Be patient and wait for him.

STELLA *(pale)*: Can you imagine! She dared keep that flower in the pocket of her apron!

THE NURSE: Well, as for me, I'm off to start the soup.

STELLA: A flower, a flower!... It's lovely. Nana, is it almost noon?

THE NURSE: Yes, little one. The apple tree's shadow is past the wall. Just a few short hours left.

STELLA: Well, that's good. *(The NURSE exits and closes the door. Alone, STELLA points the flower at the sun and sings, gaily.)*

The pleats in her skirt were three
White as snow, white as snow
And to cross the brook...

(She slips the flower into her blouse and says, very softly) Here, here, in the basket... *(She kneels again in front of the birdcage.)* Oh! Poor lonely little singer. He's waiting for his bathwater; beat wings, beat, little solid gold heart like my heart when Bruno looks at me!.. Oh, yes... *(She lies on her stomach in front of the birdcage, her elbows on the ground, her head in her hands.)*You know what? Bruno will tell me what he dreamt and I'll remember, because our dreams must be the same. *(She pretends to sob, exaggeratedly.)* Ah, Ah! Will he be back soon, my beloved? Could I live without him for even one day without dying? *(Someone knocks on the door. STELLA doesn't get up.)* Come in! *(The HERDS-MAN enters, a good-looking boy with thick hair and a smooth smile. Under his tattered cape he is dirty and healthy, calm and cheerful.)* Hello, sir.

HERDSMAN *(laughs)*: People call me Ludovicus, Ludovic, Louis.

STELLA (*smiles*): That's quite a name…

HERDSMAN (*interrupting*): Yes. I'm from Borkem, down in the valley. I came to have a letter written.

STELLA: That's right; sit down. Estrugo should be here soon.

HERDSMAN: Estrugo? He's the scribe?

STELLA: Yes.

HERDSMAN: He's not the one who can write. It's Bruno I want. Bruno writes better love letters.

STELLA: Then you'll have to come back. My husband's in town. He won't be back until noon.

HERDSMAN: Already in town? He must have left at dawn.

STELLA (*with an involuntary frown*): He left me, yesterday, after dusk.

HERDSMAN (*astonished*): He left you here alone?

STELLA (*sighs*): Yes.

HERDSMAN: And you went to bed alone?

STELLA (*simply*): Alone! And I slept, and I forgot my dream.

HERDSMAN: I'd have come if I'd known.

STELLA: Why?

HERDSMAN: To take you up the hill. That's where I spent the night, with my animals.

STELLA (*simply*): All night on the hill? Oh! No, it's too cold there.

HERDSMAN (*smiles*): I'd have kept you warm.

STELLA: I wouldn't have wanted you to.

HERDSMAN: Yes, you would. I'm as handsome as Bruno. I love you as much as he does.

STELLA *(astonished)*: You love me? Really? Since when?

HERDSMAN: Since Sunday when I saw you going to mass.

STELLA *(laughs)*: Since Sunday! Hasn't been very long!

HERDSMAN: I live all alone with my animals, and I think a lot... It can happen.

STELLA: You love me and I love Bruno. There's nothing we can do; it's nobody's fault. *(Brief pause.)* No, you're not as handsome as Bruno.

HERDSMAN: I'm younger than he is, and stronger.

STELLA *(revolted)*: Oh! Bruno's the same age as us!

HERDSMAN: The same age? He knows too much, he's educated. How can you know things and not get old? I don't even know how to write. That's why I'm here. He's going to write the letter I want to give you.

STELLA *(delighted)*: The letter is for me? But Bruno won't write it!

HERDSMAN *(confident)*: Yes, he will.

STELLA: No, he won't. Not if I tell him not to.

HERDSMAN: Go ahead. I'll offer him a suckling pig.

STELLA: Why bother? Now that I know you love me...

HERDSMAN: I have to prove it.

STELLA *(laughs)*: With words. With Bruno's words!

HERDSMAN *(furiously)*: Words belong to everyone!

STELLA: But if Bruno didn't write them for you, you couldn't prove you love me.

HERDSMAN (*calmly*): I'd carry you up the hill, without stopping to catch my breath. And when we got there I'd still have enough breath to make you shiver.

STELLA (*without malice*): Yes, you are strong. Still, you wouldn't be able to; I'm heavier than I look.

(*The HERDSMAN inches towards her with his hands out.*)

HERDSMAN: I've carried a pregnant ewe! Let me try.

STELLA (*quickly pulling back*): I'm scared of you! Let me go!… You're dirty!

HERDSMAN (*cornering her*): Stop! Come here!

STELLA: I'll scream!…

HERDSMAN: Scream all you want, I'll carry you away!

(*He catches her and lifts her up.*)

STELLA (*a loud scream*): No!

HERDSMAN (*laughing*): Yes! You weigh less in my arms than you do in my heart.

STELLA (*in cold fury, with no movement*). Put me down, you peasant!

HERDSMAN (*suddenly stubborn*): No, miss!

STELLA: I'm telling Bruno.

HERDSMAN: Tell Bruno. We'll settle it like rams, him and me. Whoever is meaner gets to keep you.

STELLA (*trembling*): Put me down.

HERDSMAN (*menacingly*): Kiss me!

(*He suddenly flips her over and says with contained fury*) And now, up the hill! No stopping for breath!

(He sets off towards the door with his burden. STELLA lets out sharp cries and struggles wildly, tearing out his curly hair.)

STELLA: Romanie! Help me! I'll bite you! Let me go! Help! Peasant, brute!

(She grabs onto the door, spinning the HERDSMAN around. He tries to back out.)

HERDSMAN *(finding this struggle funny)*: Up the hill!

STELLA: Hurry, hurry! Romanie, help!

(The NURSE comes running, armed with a stick. She smashes it against the HERDSMAN's skull and he stumbles, letting STELLA slide to the floor.)

THE NURSE: Oh! The scoundrel! What's he after, my little star? Oh, the ugly brute!

HERDSMAN *(confused, leaning up against the wall)*: Witch!

(He stays there without moving.)

THE NURSE *(kissing STELLA)*: It's my fault, all my fault. I left you alone, my turtledove. What's he after? What did he do to you?

STELLA *(looking at the HERDSMAN, who is slowly coming to his senses)*: Nana, you hit hard!

HERDSMAN *(with his eyes closed, smiles)*: Oh, no...

THE NURSE *(alarmed)*: He's not going to die on us, is he?

THE COUNT *(appears at the window wearing riding clothes)*: Did somebody scream? Was it in here? I was in the woods, just over there, and I thought I heard someone calling for help...so I tied up my horse...

THE NURSE *(curtsying)*: Good day, your lordship.

STELLA *(to the HERDSMAN)*: Get out of here.

THE COUNT: Your husband's been beating you?

THE NURSE (indignant): Oh! Your lordship! Bruno? The dear boy's been away since yesterday...

STELLA (to the HERDSMAN): Get out.

HERDSMAN (swaying): All right, but I'll be back... (He smiles.) A day in my shack and you won't be so proud. She hits hard, but not that hard; I've got a thick skull.

(He hits his head hard with both fists and laughs.) Thick! Thick! (Exits.)

STELLA (laughing): Look, he's embarrassed! Nana, you could have crushed his skull.

THE NURSE: And the next time I will, yes, I will.

STELLA (gaily): No, sir, my husband didn't beat me. And if he wanted to beat me, I'd bear it without complaining.

THE NURSE: And now I'm going to put my soup on the stove. Shut the door, Stella dear.

(After a curtsy to the COUNT, she exits right.)

THE COUNT: So you're just as much in love with him as ever?

STELLA: I never started loving him so how could I stop?

THE COUNT: You never started?

STELLA: I mean, I loved him from the first day. I was so young I don't remember it.

THE COUNT: He went into town.

STELLA: Yes, to bring back my cousin Petrus; he's the captain of a ship now.

THE COUNT: You slept alone last night?

STELLA (Has she heard?): You knew Petrus didn't you? We used to play together in the castle yard, Bruno and him and me. You would watch us for hours, peeking through the curtains.

THE COUNT: You slept alone, for the first time?

STELLA (*without malice, probably*): I think your horse is getting restless.

THE COUNT: It was you I was watching. You were tempting even then, showing off your legs...

(*STELLA laughs loudly.*)

Why are you laughing?

STELLA: I'm thinking about that boy the nurse nearly killed. He wanted to take me up the hill!

THE COUNT (*showing his teeth in an almost fierce laugh*): Ha! The fox! He chose the right hen... He'd have eaten you alive!

STELLA (*listening*): Sir, your horse is getting restless.

THE COUNT (*tight smile*): Come with me to the forest. You can ride across my saddle. Well?

STELLA (*still laughing*): The wallop he got! Ha! Ha!

THE COUNT (*sharp*): Why didn't you run to the castle, last night? I would have watched you sleep in the canopy bed. You usually curl up into your right arm, don't you? You have a mole where your garter is and another just below your waist.

STELLA (*surprised*): How... ?

THE COUNT (*showing his teeth*): ... A birthmark almost hidden under your left breast...

STELLA (*blushing*): How do you know that?

THE COUNT: When you're standing, you can touch the ground with your fingertips without bending your knees.

The Count   Stella

STELLA: Oh please, don't say any more!

THE COUNT: And you're so supple, Stella, that every morning, like a child, you bite your big toe.

(STELLA covers her face with her hands and cries nervously. The COUNT leans in and murmers with desire)

Stella! Stella! Delectable girl!

(He takes her by the hand and pulls her towards him, but she brusquely frees herself, turns around and screams.)

STELLA (deliriously): Werewolf!

(He laughs, but she grows angry.)

I used to see you behind the curtains and even then I was scared of your white teeth. Run back to the forest until Bruno traps you like a beast. The herdsman was dirty, but I liked him better than you. Your soul is as black as soot.

THE COUNT (still laughing): Don't be angry, little girl. If I had married you, you might be calling Bruno's soul black.

STELLA: How dare you? Get out, or I'll scream for Nana and her stick.

THE COUNT (still laughing): Goodbye then! So as not to offend you, dear child.

STELLA: Yes!

THE COUNT: My horse is waiting, good bye.

(He goes.)

STELLA (shouting at him as if throwing a handful of stones): I hope he throws you on your ass right in front of your castle. Your servants will snicker behind your back. Jackal! Fox!

(She spits after him.)

(She goes back inside, stamps her foot, thinks for a minute, then goes to the chimney mirror and, looking in it, prudishly tugs her shirt up and pulls her skirt down. She hides her face in her hands and murmurs indignantly.)

Oh! Oh! Oh!

(A bare-necked young MAN with tousled hair looks in at the window.)

THE MAN: Stellina.

(She spins around)

(The following passage is largely nonsense and our translation is approximate. -B.S. & A.M.)

STELLA *(with a shout of joy)*: Oh!… (*Coos.*) My da-dearest.

(She is already in his arms.)

THE MAN *(tenderly)*: Sad, sad, without you, my Stradivarius!

STELLA *(langourously)*: Hart, hart, kissies, kissies, long, hard kisses, me-loves and me-adores.

(Kisses.)

THE MAN *(quickly)*: O Columbia! Three times America! Three times new-found land! Overflow into his heart, all-enchanted, Scanavige! Lady-love, my soul's aurora borealis. Through infinity I suck up the dew in long, slow reeds and speak thanks as many times as there are blades of grass.

STELLA *(fainting)*: No.

THE MAN: The husband's not home?

STELLA *(playfully)*: No, no, he's away. He went into town yesterday, into town. (She crushes herself against him.) Have mercy, please, lay me down, over there.

THE MAN (*watching her*): Dump your harvest-moon, Stellina

STELLA (*caressingly*): ...and ice for the sick, sick girl. (*A kiss, then, plaintively*) The husband won't be back till noon. She was all alone, the shimmering girl. She slept and forgot her dream.

THE MAN: When the bad guy returns, the weeper's heart will have swifted away. Wander, wander tightrope-walker, on the cradles-rock of those who say that they love! In his soul there are long journeys to make.

STELLA (*intoxicated*): More! More!

(*They hug each other again and STELLA draws back from the window and calls:*)

Nana! Nana!

(*With one leap, the MAN jumps over the wall and is in the rom. STELLA grabs him.*)

My husband! My love!

(*The NURSE appears. STELLA calls out:*)

Look, it's Bruno! Bruno's home!

BRUNO: Hello, old Romanie!... (*He takes his cap out of his pocket.*) Catch! (*He throws it to her.*)

THE NURSE (*extremely happy*): Yes! Well! Yes, that's him, that's the man himself! He's here!

STELLA (*against him*): How we sighed this morning. Isn't he handsome, Nana?

BRUNO (*laughing, to the NURSE*): I must have gotten lost in the forest. Or there was a shipwreck. Or, at the very least I've aged since last night, right, old nurse?

THE NURSE: Oh! No, he's still handsome, but we have to clean him up, he's covered with dust!

(*She goes out at right.*)

BRUNO (*holding STELLA to him*): If you only knew how I suffered. Before I was even an hour away, I was sure I could see a glow through the pines. I almost came back to save you from the fire. Don't laugh!... And in the Black Swamp, I heard a voice, in the distance, calling me back. Maybe you'd run after me, barefoot in your nightgown. I sat down on the slope. But I knew the little girl was frightened of shadows and nighttime sounds. Oh! Mushroom-top, what secret meetings there were in the woods, what moonbeams, what spirit mirrors.

STELLA: Ooh, you're making your Thumbkin shiver. (*Now she stands back, looks at BRUNO intensely and exclaims:*) Dearest darling! I almost forgot! Is Petrus outside? (*She runs to the door.*)

BRUNO (*quickly*): No!

STELLA (*opening the door*): Petrus! Petrus is here. (*She comes back, surprised and disappointed.*) Where is he?

BRUNO: He'll be here soon.

THE NURSE (*reappearing at right with a brush in her hand*): Give me your jacket.

BRUNO: You'll see him!... (*He takes off his jacket. The nurse holds it out the window and starts brushing it off.*) Thank you, nurse... He has orders to give and orders to take. (*He sits down. Stella sinks onto his lap. He says softly:*) And me, I was so worried I couldn't wait for him. (Let me stroke your hair.) You'll see him! He's hardly changed at all, he's as honest and shy as ever. Remember? He could leapfrog over ten boys' backs, but he didn't dare look at a girl. He's still the same way—only brave when there's real danger.

STELLA (*softly*): Florence brought me your primrose, a little late. It's here in the basket.

BRUNO: Petrus is captain of a three-master that sings in the wind like a forest of poplars. What a man! He sails round the world on rough seas. He'll tell you himself. He's still a young man, but he's known all kinds of weather.

THE NURSE: Put your jacket back on, child, and get up.

(*BRUNO and STELLA get up. The NURSE kneels and brushes the young*) *man's pants.)*

BRUNO: Now Petrus will rest for six months. Stella, you'll get his room ready. The one next to ours.

STELLA *(opens her eyes wide with astonishment)*: The room upstairs? Next to ours?

BRUNO *(laughs)*: Yes, yes, what does it matter? He needs to feel cared-for and close to us after being alone for so long. He'll be here soon. Make the room a little messy so he doesn't find it too still.

STELLA: Yes, my love.

THE NURSE: This is dust from the sunken path. I know it; it sticks to cloth like dye.

BRUNO: He's coming in a coach.

(The scribe ESTRUGO appears at the door at left. He seems at once attentive and distracted. When he speaks, there's always a slight hesitation, but then his words come quickly, too quickly. His gestures are like a trampoline for his words. When unable to express himself, his gestures remain suspended for a long periods. BRUNO welcomes him gaily.)

And here's our good Estrugo, the ever-faithful Estrugo! Hello, Estrugo.

ESTRUGO: Hello Bruno. How did your trip go?

BRUNO: About ten miles yesterday into town; as much again this morning coming home. About what the farmers going to market do every day. Stella has been through a lot. *(ESTRUGO is about to ask a question, but he's too late— STELLA has already thrown herself into BRUNO's arms. He adds:)* I imagined her burned, drowned, strangled, lost! Stella, go get the room ready for Petrus. And you, Estrugo, go to your desk, we need your loveliest script. *(STELLA and the NURSE remain side by side, gaping at Bruno.)*

ESTRUGO: The mayor is right behind me. He's going to ask you for a proclamation.

BRUNO: Excellent. And I'll ask for a wide ribbon for Stella in return.

(STELLA runs to him immediately.) She likes moiré ribbons, don't you, Starlight? And boxes of soap and lacey paper? Go on, Stella.

STELLA *(leaving reluctantly)*: Yes, my love.

BRUNO *(to ESTRUGO)*: We have other tasks. Count Morten is selling his land and his castle. He wishes the sale to be announced in terms finer than numbers and lines and dots. He requests a decription of the terrain, a landscape-painting-in-words.

ESTRUGO *(sincerely)*: In verse?

BRUNO: Almost. You'll see.

(ESTRUGO is at his desk. The old NURSE has been sweeping the ground, picking up the dust from BRUNO's clothes.)

STELLA *(tenderly)*: Well then Bruno, adieu. Adieu, adieu, we're always parting.

BRUNO *(softly)*: And always coming together again!

(A kiss.)

STELLA *(sniffling)*: Oh kisses that go round the world three times, and the Ho Ho Ho and the Tum Tum Tum.

(The MAYOR enters. A fat man; sweaty and out of breath.)

THE NURSE *(exiting at right)*: And I'll put a chicken on the spit in honor of Bruno. And Petrus, too.

MAYOR: Greetings to all here present and to come!

STELLA *(curtsying)*: Your Honor.

(She goes out smiling to herself. The two men watch her climb the stairs in silence. When she gets to the landing, the young woman turns, smiles sweetly, gives a very low curtsy and leaves by the door at right.)

BRUNO *(to the MAYOR, proudly)*: Isn't she the daintiest, most graceful creature you ever saw? She could walk on water without getting her little feet wet!

MAYOR *(with a loud, incredulous laugh)*: Oh! Oh! No! ...

BRUNO *(astonished)*: You don't think so? I do. She carries herself with such elegance!... She's as graceful as a swan! Do you know what gives that spring to her walk? It's because her heels hardly touch the ground, and her legs are long and straight, and her chest is small and her breasts are high. She's not mortal! She's a sprite! *(He adds, with conviction and very seriously:)* I carry her in my heart the way a kangaroo carries a baby in its pouch.

MAYOR *(laughs)*: Oh! Oh! No!...

BRUNO *(to the scribe)*: Estrugo, write. Two sheets of paper, one for the proclamation, the other to announce the sale. I'll dictate them at the same time. Petrus is coming and I want to finish before he arrives. *(To the MAYOR, with a persuasive smile:)* Yes, like a kangaroo...

MAYOR *(confidentially)*: I need your help... Mum's the word!... There are still raids on the forest. They cut down ten saplings the other night in the Wood-of-the-Heartless-Woman. Listen: I don't want to be unpopular. Not here and not in the county. There must be a proclamation against cutting down trees... and yet we have to allow it... *(puts his finger to one side of his nose)* only we can't be involved. Find an angle. Mum's the word!

BRUNO *(dictating to ESTRUGO)*: "The castle of the counts of Morten, built high up on a cliff, overlooks the fair, deep valley of the Mieuvre."

MAYOR: Listen carefully: these people also like to poach, they enjoy that. You see... Mum's the word! Mum's the word!... But as far as the governor of the province is concerned, I'm beyond reproach, eh?... Quite the opposite.

BRUNO *(to ESTRUGO)*: "Dear citizens. Despite the vigilance of our officials, felons have once again brazenly assaulted our land." (Am I going too fast?)

(He takes the MAYOR by the arm.)

Stella's so supple that—would you believe it?—she can twist around like ivy and touch her neck to her ankle. She's an acrobat... We play children's games. She can touch the floor with her fingertips without bending her knees. I love her madly!

ESTRUGO: "Assaulted our land..."

BRUNO *(dictating)*: Between Sunday night and Monday morning, the vandals attacked…"

(He turns to the MAYOR.)

Twenty trees? Thirty? Fifty?

MAYOR: Ten…

BRUNO *(decisively)*: "One hundred trees, in the Wood-of-the-Heartless-Woman."

MAYOR *(puffing)*: Aha! Yes! Mum's the word! I understand! Now they can cut down… Shh!

BRUNO: "To preserve the safety of the community, it is crucial that strict surveillance be organized without delay." (Write.) When she curtsied just now, did you notice how she bent her knees just like a doe?

MAYOR *(shocked)*: No, I didn't.

BRUNO *(calling)*: Stella! Stella! Look more closely this time! I'll have her bend over a little more so you can admire her legs… Stella!

(STELLA appears at the landing.)

STELLA: You called, my love?

BRUNO *(pretending not to see her, dictates quickly to ESTRUGO)*: Write! Write! "From the turrets of the building, which in times past dominated the enemy duchy of Meng, the view extends over the southern forests and the plains, all the way to the sea and the horizon beyond."

STELLA: My love, you called?

BRUNO *(tenderly)*: It's you! Yes, my heart, yes. I had this desperate need to see you for a moment. And here you are, and I'm happy… Don't move. No, don't come down! Kisses!

STELLA *(smiles a sad smile)*: From so far away!

BRUNO: Don't be sad. Go now, my little star. Soon I won't let you go.

STELLA *(sighs)*: Farewell, my love.

(She goes out slowly.)

BRUNO *(exalted)*: She hovers like a beautiful shadow over my life. Ah! This love fills my soul to overflowing. Now tell me, don't those legs of hers have incomparable style? The contours of her ankles taper so subtly that your eyes seem to be present at their very creation, ah!... Then the line of her calf, so soft yet so strong, a marvelous trajectory stretching miraculously to her knee. There your gaze stops and you think that, having reached such heights, the line will content itself with that careless grace. But no! I tell you, at its extremity, it effortlessly rebounds, bends with the purity of an astral cycle, and, without the slightest strain, traces her suspended buttocks, ah! ah!... Do you understand?

MAYOR *(shocked)*: No.

BRUNO *(with increasing exaltation)*: Yes, yes, that same line curves towards the sweep of her scented back, rises gently to her shoulders, reaches towards the nape of her neck, encloses her hair in its cunning arabesques and, arriving at her face, becomes a sign almost divine, arcs under her bold chin, flows langorously down her ample neck and then, suddenly, is caught up in the movement of gathering the swelling breast of her innocent youth! At last, broken for the first and last time, this line unfurls over a stomach as pure as the sheen of gold, and then loses itself like a wave on the beach!

ESTRUGO: "...that strict surveillance be organized without delay."

BRUNO *(carried away)*: And that's just one line, one single line! And there are thousands of lines like it. What am I saying? Hundreds of thousands. Millions, depending on your perspective, and each line as perfect as the one before, and all gathered together in bundles, festooned, curved, undulating, straight or twisted, plump or slender, rising or falling, vibrant or languid, stretched out or bunched together, rolled, rippled, crinkled, knotted, swollen, tightly wound, sharp or blurry, caressing or shaking or wavy, spiral, helical, spun, one after another or at once, all these lines go in one direction, just one, bringing love into my heart.

ESTRUGO: " ...all the way to the sea and the horizon beyond."

BRUNO: Her beauty so moves me that I'm out of breath!

(Without pausing, he dictates to ESTRUGO.)

"I invite my fellow citizens to form a twenty-four-hour village watch made up of men between the ages of fifteen and sixty. They will take turns performing this task."

MAYOR *(overcome with joy)*: Mum's the word! Mum's the word!

BRUNO: "The watch will wear badges and may carry double-barreled shotguns."

(The MAYOR sits down and exhales deeply.)

MAYOR: Ah! Ah! Excellent! Everybody's happy! Mum's the word! There'll be fire and blood on all sides.

BRUNO: You'll send me colored ribbons for Stella. Ribbons are her weakness.

MAYOR: Ah! Ah! I can just see them, the poor buggers. Marching in pairs through the forest at midnight. What a job they'll make of it!

BRUNO: If you could only see Stella at midnight! Her snow-white feet, her knees—rosy and eloquent like a shy girl's face—and above all that, her delicious warm skin: like dough. If only you could see her birthmark, right there, a blemish that makes her flesh seem more tender! Small, high, girlish breasts!

(The HERDSMAN looks in at the back door.)

HERDSMAN: Hello.

BRUNO: Hello.

HERDSMAN *(smiling calmly)*: I'm Ludovic from Borkem. You're back? Can you write a letter for me?

BRUNO: Yes, I'll do it tomorrow. Are you in love? What should it say?

HERDSMAN: That.

ESTRUGO: "...They will take turns performing this task."

MAYOR *(triumphantly, to ESTRUGO)*: "The watch will wear badges and may carry double-barreled shotguns." Ah! Ah! It's perfect.

BRUNO *(to the HERDSMAN)*: What's her name?

HERDSMAN: Stella.

BRUNO *(naively)*: The same as my wife. Do they look alike?

HERDSMAN *(simply)*: It's your wife I love.

BRUNO *(laughs)*: Ha!

HERDSMAN: She's the one. You don't want to write the letter?

BRUNO *(amused)*: Why not? You can come and get it tomorrow.

HERDSMAN *(defiantly)*: No need. You can give it to her for me. You won't?

BRUNO: I'll give it to her, I promise.

HERDSMAN: Swear.

BRUNO: I swear.

HERDSMAN *(astonished)*: You're not afraid?

BRUNO *(laughs)*: Of course not!

(The HERDSMAN looks at him in astonishment.)

MAYOR *(taking the proclamation)*: And now, my signature!

(The door opens and PETRUS enters. BRUNO rushes to him, the two men embrace in silence, then, also in silence, they gaze at each other.)

HERDSMAN: I'll bring you a suckling pig... Thank you... .

(He goes.)

MAYOR *(waving the proclamation)*: I'll post this in its place, on the door of

Town Hall, and have it read out in the market place... This is excellent!

(He sees PETRUS.)

Wait a minute! Don't I know you?

BRUNO *(emotionally)*: This is Stella's cousin Petrus.

MAYOR *(on his way out)*: Oh, yes!... Now I remember. Good bye, boys.

BRUNO *(yelling after him)*: The ribbons!

(Once the MAYOR has gone he turns to ESTRUGO.)

Estrugo, why don't you take a walk.

(Then he turns to PETRUS with an air of profound cordiality.)

I'm so happy. You're back with us. Does the town seem changed?

(ESTRUGO goes.)

PETRUS: It looks smaller to me, more cramped, but familiar all the same, humble and cheerful. The sunken road didn't frighten me the way it used to.

BRUNO *(without raising his voice)*: And Stella, just wait till you see her! She's getting your room ready—the one next to ours. Just wait till you see her! You're moved! I'm trembling as if I were the one coming back. She was fourteen when you left, wasn't she? She was pretty then... But wait till you see her now!

PETRUS *(smiling)*: How we used to fight.

BRUNO *(still speaking softly)*: That won't happen now. I won't call her yet. Let me tell you some more about her. Are you looking at the house?

PETRUS: Yes. I remember nothing except the landing. We hauled in the sacks through that window. That's where the granary was...such a huge space. Flour poured out of every crack.

BRUNO: Now that's our bedroom, Stella's room. She'll seem more beautiful to you now, the little Estelle we used to play with. She's grown taller, and at the same time she's filled out. Wait till you see her! You know I was already in love with her back then. And since then my love has only grown. It weighs me down more and more, every day, every minute, and it becomes more precious. Am I boring you, Petrus?

PETRUS (*with feeling*): Certainly not!

BRUNO (*passionately*): My love is like a child nursing at it's mother's breast. It grows, Petrus! I feed it with all my being. What do you think, can it last? Stella is so good, too, so devoted to my future. Her soul... Wait till you see her! (*Calling loudly:*) Stella, Stella! Hurry up, Stellina! (*He hurries over to PETRUS and stands next to him, waiting.*) Stella! (*STELLA appears at the top of the stairs; pauses; then lets out a little cry of joy and astonishment.*)

STELLA: Oh, Petrus, you're here!

PETRUS (*affectionately*): Hello, Stella.

STELLA (*comes down quickly*): He's not covered in medals. But you *are* a captain. Hello, Petrus.

BRUNO: Give each other a kiss!

(*He pushes PETRUS towards STELLA. They kiss, clumsily.*)

STELLA (*intimidated*): We were sworn enemies once....

PETRUS (*smiling*): That made things easier....

BRUNO: Come here, Stella. (*STELLA presses against him. Her points her towards PETRUS.*) See? He hasn't changed! His eyes are a little lighter, from staring at the sea, but that's all. He still has that wild look.

STELLA: Where are your bags?

PETRUS: They're bringing them later.

BRUNO (*brusquely*): Well, Petrus? Tell me what you think! Did I lie?

PETRUS (*smiling*): Stella is very pretty....

BRUNO (*gloating*): And nimble and lively and light!... Stella, curtsy for us... yes... now take three steps towards the door, yes... now come back (Look at her, Petrus!). Now spin around.

STELLA (*smiling, astonished*): What for?

BRUNO (*carried away*): Give me your hand.

(*He takes STELLA's hand and spins her around.*)

Spin, Stella! Waltz! Isn't she an excellent dancer? Her walk is as calm as a sleeper's breath! She leaves a trail of light in her wake. She sways like a buoy in the bay. Oh! Petrus!

(*He lets go of STELLA, runs to PETRUS, puts a hand on his shoulder and looks him straight in the eye.*)

Am I boring you, Petrus?

PETRUS (*smiling*): You love her, my boy.

BRUNO: If you only knew... Listen, Petrus, you're my friend... no, I can't explain it well...

(*He turns towards STELLA. He is determined.*)

Stella, my flower, my little princess... show him your legs.

STELLA (*with a cry*): Oh!

BRUNO: I beg you, lift your skirt a little.

STELLA (*blushing but without shame*): Oh, no!

BRUNO: Petrus is your cousin and my friend. I want him to see how lovely you are!... Lift your skirt, dearest, lift it.

(*STELLA, lowering her head, slowly lifts her skirt.*)

Look, Petrus! A cornucopia, a field of lilies, the purity of a Grecian vase. (See how lucky I am!) Higher, Stella, higher! Lift your skirt a little higher. You see,

Petrus!

PETRUS *(not laughing)*: You love her, Bruno.

BRUNO: Listen to me Stella, my little nymph, lift it above the knee. Let yourself appear to him as you must in dreams. Ah! Ah! Ah! What do you say now, Petrus?

(STELLA lets her skirt fall and BRUNO kisses the hem as it falls. Then he gets up and clasps STELLA close.)

As clear as dew! As fresh as moonlight in the forest! And elegant, and supple, and consoling.

(He feverishly unbuttons the young woman's blouse.)

STELLA *(shocked)*: Oh! My love!

BRUNO: Your breast, your little swollen pearl!

STELLA: No!

PETRUS *(violently)*: Bruno, you love her too much!

BRUNO *(impetuously)*: I love you both! Let him say if he has seen on any tropical beach a shell more finely wrought, more pleasing to the eye! Her breasts, her little innocent breast, her tender little breasts. *(He uncovers STELLA's breasts. She hides her face in the crook of her arm. BRUNO leaps towards PETRUS, exulting.)*

Did I lie? Did I exaggerate by even a hair? Say something, answer me... but above all look, look...

STELLA *(in a tender and plaintive whisper)*: My love...

(Deep silence.)

(PETRUS looks openly. BRUNO's eyes never leave his cousin's impassive face.)

(Suddenly, for no apparent reason, he slaps PETRUS hard. All three of them cry out.)

(STELLA crumbles onto the couch, in a near faint.)

(PETRUS hasn't time to recover before BRUNO grabs him and immobilizes him in a tight embrace.)

BRUNO *(panting)*: Petrus, for God's sake, don't hit me back!... What's happening to us? Let's not fight like animals.

PETRUS *(immobile, furious)*: You are a madman! A madman!

BRUNO: Remember, we used to play together. We gave as good as we got.

PETRUS *(calming down)*: A madman!

BRUNO *(without loosening his grip)*: Forgive me; I thought I saw your eyes light up!... It's the first time I've had this feeling. Promise you won't attack me. Tell me we're not going to roll on the floor and tear each other to pieces. I love you like a brother. Where did that burning feeling come from? Your room is ready. Please say you'll stay with us, please.

PETRUS *(subdued)*: Fine. Let me go. If it had been anyone else, I'd have killed him.

(The old NURSE appears. She sees the two men clasped together.)

NURSE: Petrus is here? And nobody told me? Heavens, look at them! How they love each other!

(BRUNO lets go of PETRUS.)

Hello, child. You have a pretty cap now.

PETRUS *(kissing her on the forehead)*: How are you, old nurse? Sharp as ever? Still gossiping away?

NURSE: Yes, you old rascal, yes, but my teeth aren't what they were. I bet you've seen redskins and black men.

(BRUNO has gone to STELLA, who regains her composure and takes him in her arms. All four speak at once.)

(Together:)

STELLA: Oh, the bad boy. He's frightened his one and only. No more sweet flowers.

PETRUS: Yes, and Americans and pygmy monkeys. I'll show you on the map, Nana.

BRUNO: My own little dwarf, my compass, my cream, my dancing Indian priestess!

NURSE: And you'll tell me whether my chicken is tender. It's roasting over lovely hot coals...

(A sudden silence.)

BRUNO: There. We're all better. Stella, show Petrus to his room.

STELLA: Come, cousin. You haven't seen the new windows; they frame such pretty pictures. Yours has a field, with half a red roof showing and the branch of a cherry tree against the sky.

NURSE: I'll go with you and help him get settled.

(STELLA goes upstairs, followed by PETRUS and the old woman.)

You've been ironing your trousers by putting them under the mattress, my son.

PETRUS *(laughing)*: That's right. And I don't even sleep in a bed every night.

STELLA: My window looks out on the orchard and two trembling poplars...

(They vanish upstairs.

BRUNO has been sitting in an armchair, exhausted.

Long silence. The sound of laughter comes from above.

Finally ESTRUGO appears at the street door.)

BRUNO *(glumly)*: Estrugo, sit down there. No, over here, come closer. Shh!

Wait, shh! shh! Shut up! Will you shut up?! *(Silence. Then he asks bitterly, without looking at ESTRUGO:)* Tell me, do you think Stella is faithful to me? *(Dry laugh.)* Ah! Ah! What a question! Yes, answer me straight. Faithful or not faithful, yes or no? Why do I ask this...? *(ESTRUGO has no chance to answer. His gestures are suspended. BRUNO answers for him.)* She's as faithful as the sky is blue. Today! As the earth turns. *(Illumination:)* Yes! *(Then, dark again.)* No comparisons, if you please. Answer yes or no. Faithful? Prove it! *(He gets up.)* Ah! I've got you there! You can't prove it. Liar! You'd swear she was? Swear. You don't dare? *(He gets carried away.)* He swears! He swears, poor man. If you don't swear, then you're saying one *could* have doubts. About everything? Yes, but not about Stella... *(Furious:)* It's too much. Don't defend her. Shut up! Be quiet!... *(Silence. BRUNO, beside himself:)* I don't know. This anguish came upon me so suddenly. I thought I saw Petrus' eyes light up. The way he looked at her! Yes, yes, Petrus! He lives alone. But should I doubt him, too? He seemed so loyal, he held himself in check, that's a good sign... A woman is clever and cunning enough to spin a web of trust and purity around herself. No, not Stella; other women, no doubt... *(He gets carried away.)* Doesn't Stella have two eyes in her head, two arms, two legs and the mark of an umbilical cord? Why do you always lie? *(He calms down a little, complains:)* Yes, I'm going mad. I can't see clearly. *(He sits back down.)* Estrugo! Answer me! Is it wise to have Petrus stay in the house, so close to an impressionable young woman? (You know how naïve and sensitive she is!) Without them even meaning it, love could creep up on them softly. Well? Could they resist? They don't even have to go that far to lose control of their imaginations. Soon an evil thought appears. If not the thought, the hope, the dream! Ah! You see! In their sleep they will construct a dream made out of tiny shared moments, they'll draw them around themselves and me! Well? Then the next day in spite of themselves, an intimate complicity... How will they act when they wake and they meet again? And I... *(He gets up and shivers.)* Is it possible that all Stella's thoughts have always been about me? That feverish nights never dampened them, never? *(He shouts suddenly, quite loudly:)* Estrugo, I am a cuckold! *(Then, he calls out madly:)* Stella! Stella! Come down! Stella! I'm calling you! *(To ESTRUGO:)* Your silence is confession enough. Yes, yes, I understand. Stella! Stella!

STELLA *(appearing on the balcony)*: Here I am, my love.

BRUNO *(barely restraining himself)*: You're in no hurry.

(ESTRUGO tries to get up. BRUNO stops him.) Stay!

STELLA (*gracefully*): Oh! Yes, I am, my love.

BRUNO (*tightly*): Sit down there.

(*They are sitting so as to form a small triangle. BRUNO at back, STELLA and ESTRUGO face to face.*)

STELLA (*gaily*): You've invented a new game? Estrugo is playing, too! Ah! It must be a riddle!

BRUNO (*deliberately*): Tell me something you can't tell me.

STELLA (*considers, then:*): "Cat's got my tongue."

BRUNO (*sharply*): What did you do last night after I left?

STELLA: I hung out the window and watched until you were out of sight.

BRUNO: No, you didn't.

STELLA: I did.

BRUNO: No, that's not the right answer.

STELLA (*amused*): You're trying to trap me! Ha! Ha! Cat's got my tongue, cat's got my tongue!

BRUNO: Tell me something you did that you weren't supposed to do.

STELLA: I slept and I forgot my dream.

BRUNO (*startled*): Your dream?

STELLA (*clapping*): You caught me!

BRUNO (*dryly*): Not yet. This morning?

STELLA: Cornelia was here...

BRUNO (*angry*): Something you can't tell me!

STELLA: The herdsman...

BRUNO: I already know. He's in love with you. He told me. Something you can't tell me.

STELLA: The count...

BRUNO *(furious)*: Something. You. Can't. Tell. Me! I'm not laughing, you fool!

STELLA *(taken aback)*: Oh! My god, it wasn't a riddle! *(She starts crying.)* My love, when you undid my blouse before, your primrose fell out and I stepped on it and crushed it.

BRUNO: If you dare tell me all this, then it must be something you *can* tell me! *(He gets up, cold and energetic.)* Estrugo, go upstairs. You are my true friend, you didn't try to keep my misfortune from me. Go. Tell Petrus to leave. I won't have him in the house another minute. Go. *(To STELLA:)* Be quiet! *(To ESTRUGO.)* Are you going? You're quicker to hurt me than to help...

(ESTRUGO, after many attempts to protest, goes upstairs.)

STELLA *(afraid)*: Oh! Bruno, my only hope, what kind of madness is this? I'll make you better...

BRUNO *(darkly)*: I'll be better when Petrus is gone.

STELLA *(at once)*: Then he should go! *(Mournfully.)* But have you caught some fever he brought with him from the tropics? Who could have dreamed—? You were so strong before he came. You don't love me anymore?

BRUNO: I love you too much! I love you too much! That's what Petrus saw!

STELLA: Then tell me what's the matter!... Tell me what's wrong. What herbs should I pick to soothe you with? Should I laugh, smile, kneel, dance?

BRUNO *(dryly)*: You should shut up.

STELLA *(crying)*: Are you punishing me because I crushed your flower?

BRUNO *(seeing PETRUS approach, he lowers his voice)*: Quiet! If you want to please me!... Don't ask any questions! Don't answer any either!

(Silence.)

(PETRUS comes down, followed by the NURSE and ESTRUGO. He stops at the foot of the stair.)

PETRUS: Bruno, you've done a wrong thing. I forgive you, you're not right in the head. *(In the silence that follows, he crosses the room. To STELLA.)* Goodbye, Stella.

NURSE: But why is he leaving? Stay with us, child. You won't taste my chicken?

PETRUS *(smiles)*: Thank you, nurse. You are a good soul. Bruno, I forgive you.

(He goes.)

(Silence.)

NURSE *(overcome)*: Oh! Oh! Oh! What a mess. I don't understand it at all. I'll go and set the table. Such a nice chicken...

(She goes.)

BRUNO *(at once overcome with tearful remorse)*: Estrugo! You chased him away! I'll never forget what you did!... Yes, and I know you'll answer... You don't just let someone drown!... It was bad enough you standing by, and then to obey me?... I'd a thousand times rather have received that blow myself... Estrugo, you have poisoned my life. You've made me doubt Petrus. And you see: like a porcupine in retreat, he shot me with a poisoned quill. Shut up! Shut up! You made me doubt myself and Stella... Now get out!

STELLA *(dissolving in tears)*: Oh! Estrugo, wicked man! Why have you plotted against us?

(She sits down. BRUNO comes to with a jolt.)

BRUNO *(furious)*: Why are you crying? For what? For whom? Who are you crying for?

CURTAIN

ACT 2

(The same room.

The shutters on the lower windows are closed. A warm gold light comes in from above.

Silence.

From outside comes the sound of keys clinking.

The door cracks open. BRUNO pokes in his head. He inspects the room and then enters, followed by ESTRUGO.)

BRUNO *(in a low voice, speaking quickly)*: The door! Shut the door! There. Nobody followed us down the street? Come here. Lock the door. Are you sure no one followed us? Get over here! Is the door shut tight? – Oh! Estrugo, I am not happy. Put your hat over the keyhole. Sit down. There's no need to check on Stella. She'll be right where I left her, flat on the floor. She's obedient, but it's a ruse.

(Nevertheless he goes to the door on the left and puts his eye to the keyhole.)

(Returning.) Exactly.

Estrugo, you know how happy I was. We'd been promised to one other since we were children.
Aren't you hot?… I can't remember the last time the sun was this harsh. It crackles outside like a chestnut on the fire. The only bearable place today is the cemetery. There's shade there and there are birds.
(He sits down next to ESTRUGO. He lowers his voice still more.)

Will people think it's strange that the shutters are closed? We're just protecting ourselves from the heavens…

(Silence. Is he dreaming? No, he's waiting.)

Well, I'm listening. *(Bitterly.)* I'm listening. Don't spare me, you're my only friend. You love me, don't you, dear Estrugo? Scorch me, trample my heart, corrode it, burn, twist, tear, pierce, pinch, punch, shrink, kill, kill me! I'm brave.

What did you want to tell me?

(Growing angry. Still in a low voice.)

You don't want to talk? You refuse to betray her? And yet you say you love me! Have we gone this far together for you to keep quiet now? Maybe you're her accomplice? You've sworn an oath of secrecy?

(All of a sudden, quickly.)

Or did you only promise? You can break a promise. You're not bound by a promise. She'll forgive you for giving away a trivial detail…. Now that you've started, finish it off! Don't leave me in agony!

You don't dare tell me? It's that bad? Oh, he must really love me! He knows how tormented I'll be. Don't worry, dear friend, tell me. I'm ready for the pain. Confess! When did you see her? When did you pledge yourself to silence?

(He rises angrily.)

Could you have come while I was away? Would you dare? But no… She went out that night and you saw her with her lover.

(He shakes his fist at the door. A cry of desperation.)

Oh! You wanton she-goat! I'll make you circle round and round your stake! And then I'll shorten your rope!

(Regaining control of himself.)

Wait, I'm getting nowhere. My sighs just blow the anger out of my heart. There! Where did you see her?

(Not even listening.)

I slept under a huge weight last night. The imprint of my body on the fleece of my mattress was deeper than ever before. A mountainous sleep! Taking advantage of me in my senseless state, she slipped out of bed.

How did she get out of the house? Did she tell you? No! She defies you, too. She knows how devoted you are to me.

The keys to the doors and shutters were under my pillow. I'm sure she would have taken them, but my head was too heavy. Not even a man could have lifted it!

How could she have gotten out without keys? Ah, she's diabolically clever!

Do you think a woman could change into a mouse and scurry under the door?

(Quickly, bitterly.)

She can, she can! I tell you she can! She's made of different stuff from us... Otherwise, how?

Listen: do you think that by stacking one table on top of another and then a chair on top of that and then a small stool on the chair, I could reach the bullseye window in my room?

(He leaps up.)

You're right! That's it! That's how she got out! Ah! The slut! Unbelievable woman! A woman so fine, so accomplished, dear friend. When I picture her naked, undoing her hair, my heart breaks open.

And he, he, was he waiting outside with a ladder? How else could she get down to the orchard from the roof? Could you jump from there without breaking your leg? Could you slide down the ivy without tearing it off the wall? Can she walk on fog, along a moonbeam, does she have wings—do you think I'm crazy?

(He trembles.)

Oh! You hit me where it hurts. Why did you tell me all this?

(ESTRUGO makes a helpless gesture.)

Quiet! Speak more softly!... You're right, I have no reason to be upset with you... You think only of my honor... But your words ferment in me.

Yes, I hear her: don't worry, she won't know you've confided in me.

(He lowers his voice still more.) I had a dream, dear Estrugo, I dreamed he was at the far edge of the orchard. He was carrying her in his arms.

(Hiccups and grimaces with disgust.)

Hic! And he set her down in the prairie, on the other side of the hedge. Hic!

And she ran barefoot in the wet grass until they reached the woods where the shadows hid them. Hic! Hic! Hic!

Don't nod your head like a turkey! Tell me this, do dreams come true? Not always? Not often? Sometimes? Do they ever come true? Could they come true just once? Once would be enough!

Why pretend they wouldn't go to the woods? Answer, unless your tongue is stuck in your mouth like a pit in a peach!

Ah! So there we are. I'm not deaf! Oh! The whore! I will ration her bread and water, her light and sun! What drink did she give me yesterday that made me sleep like that?

Estrugo, if you could only see her when I question her, her expression so naïve, her eyes so bright... Estrugo, if you knew how perfect her body is, her serene breasts, her long silky legs, you'd doubt that her soul was deformed.

(Overcome with fury.)

The bitch! The bitch!... Someone else has had her! I'm sure that the instant he left her, he went to the tavern to squander my treasure: to boast of her smooth gold skin, to tell whether she laughs in pleasure or weeps! And all the while I'm crushed by sleep after drinking her poppyseed potion.

Go away! Go away! Your look strips me naked. I want to hide from the eyes of men. Go.

(ESTRUGO gets up.)

No, stay a bit longer. Tell me his name. Yes, her lover's name. You won't tell me!? Then go to hell!... Get out!

(He calls him back again.)

Estrugo, for God's sake, finish me off. His name!

Get out! Get out! Stay away from me, Judas, liar! You'd tell me she's innocent, she who, the better to fool me, puts on airs of sincerity, she who hid with him (his name! his name!) in some dark shadow. With him! She who ran in her nightgown over the lawn, who escaped out the bullseye window, went down the ladder, almost poisoned me, whose secret you are keeping!

(Quickly, in a soft voice, pushing ESTRUGO towards the door.)

Shh! Shh! All right, I understand. You can count on me, I'll be silent as the grave. Silence... I understand. You've said nothing, nothing at all.

Wait. If you find out more details of her orgy, let me know. Good bye, dear Estrugo, faithful friend.

Just take a stroll around the house; I'll be needing you.

(He pushes ESTRUGO out and closes the door to the street.)

(He immediately runs to the other door, opens it and yells with anger and scorn.)

Here, fiend, here, witch!... Here, toad! Sow! Bitch! Here, child of apes and whatever with fish tails! Here, daughter of an icy serpent and an apple with a rotten core. Come here, woman! Woman, do you hear me?

Stella!

(Stella appears, dressed in a black cape with the hood up. Her face is covered by a grotesque carboard mask.)

STELLA *(softly)*: Here I am, my love.

BRUNO: What took you so long, monster? I was calling you, whore!

STELLA: Were you really calling me by all those names?

BRUNO: Yes, yes, you and no other. Stubborn liar, shameless slut, yes, you. Didn't you recognize yourself?

What were you doing when I got home? What did you do while I was away? What, who, were you thinking about?

Answer me!

STELLA: You're not giving me a chance to, my love.

BRUNO: What you want is a chance to think. But it's not me you're thinking about! You're stalling for a chance to dream up more schemes and malicious plots. Now you've found it, haven't you?

(Abruptly.)

Who's that behind you?

STELLA: No one, my love.

BRUNO: There's someone behind you. Stop! Don't move!

(He circles her.)

Vixen! She can make him circle round her like the shadow on a sundial.

(He is in front of her now.)

Crouch down.

(She obeys. He looks over her head.)

Get up! Where is he?

Why is your dress spread out like a bell? Take off your coat. *(She takes off her coat.)* Lift your skirt. *(She lifts her skirt. He is indignant.)* Ah! Drop your skirt, drop it! A peeled frog has more modesty.

(He sits down trembling.)

Oh! My god, what suffering! She allows me no rest. She's capable of the meanest tricks.

STELLA *(leaning against him, consoling him)*: Oh! Bruno, if my crime is loving you, I deserve a terrible punishment. You couldn't make me suffer enough. And if my death would soothe you, let me die right away...

BRUNO *(pushes her away)*: Don't take that doleful tone with me, you siren.

STELLA: How can I help it?

BRUNO: Where did you go last night?

STELLA: Last night I slept pressed against you, my love.

BRUNO *(gets up, irritated)*: Ah! That poisonous tongue! Every word you speak is a snare. Against me, you said it, "against me": speak against me, act against me, fight against my rest, sleep against me and at me, yes, you said it yourself! If you were sleeping, what did you dream about?

STELLA *(sudden laugh)*: Oh! I had such a strange dream! Imagine—I was in my underwear...

BRUNO *(interrupts her, furious)*: ...In your nightgown! In your nightgown! Liar! Last night you left the room in your nightgown!

STELLA: How could I leave? Aren't the keys always under your pillow?

BRUNO: So? How do you know they're there? You know it very well, it seems. Couldn't you open the door without keys? You're trying to make a fool of me. And couldn't you steal my ring of keys, while I was having nightmares from the drink you gave me. Yes! Yes! Your drink... or some other drug?

STELLA: Oh! What drug! I swear to you that I didn't get out of bed until morning.

BRUNO: And I swear to you that you climbed the wall like a monkey to get to the bullseye window…

STELLA: Oh! No, my love.

BRUNO: …that a ladder was waiting there…

STELLA: No…

BRUNO: …that you went through the orchard…

STELLA: No!

BRUNO: …and that you got tangled up with some fox in the midnight shadows…

STELLA: No! No!

BRUNO: …and that I'll strangle you!

Don't tell me no. Man knows falsehood because a beautiful creature once tricked him… Don't tell me no! Your doll face is a perfect lie. Your real face is that monster's mask. Keep it on! Let its hideous expression sear your flesh so no one will ever again be fooled by your modest smile. Don't keep telling me no. It was by saying no that you made me resentful and bitter.

(He sits back down, exhausted.)

STELLA *(with effort)*: Yes, my love.

BRUNO: I've lost all my youth and half my mind.

STELLA: Yes, my love.

BRUNO: I am exhausted, sunk, a weight to myself and to others.

STELLA: Yes, my love.

BRUNO *(weakly)*: Ah! She's killing me!… "Yes, my love," and I'm dead!

STELLA *(frightened)*: Bruno! Come back, my only love, my dearest hope.

BRUNO *(pushing her away)*: Away! Tell me your lover's name.

STELLA: Alas!

BRUNO: His name! It's John the wheelwright's son?

STELLA *(repeats passively)*: It's John…

BRUNO: No! It's Hector from the shipping office?

STELLA: It's Hector…

BRUNO: No, he's too fat. It's Allan who fishes down by the river?

STELLA: It's Allan, the fisherman...

BRUNO: No, no, he's too dull. It's Paul the farrier.

STELLA: Paul, the...

BRUNO: He's too dirty and he spits. The town clerk?

STELLA: The town clerk.

BRUNO: Or Christopher from the barbershop on Green Street?

STELLA: Christopher from the barbershop on Green Street.

BRUNO: Or "the-gentleman-who-speaks-to-the-lady-when-he-goes-to-the-castle-on-Sunday..."?

STELLA: The-gentleman-who-speaks-to-the-lady-when-he...

BRUNO (desperate, finished): None of them! Not one of these men!... She won't confess!

STELLA: I will no longer say yes or no, my love, so as not to torment you. It shall be as you wish. But for God's sake, please don't hold back your beloved anger, kill me now!

(She falls to her knees and sobs beneath her mask.)

BRUNO (embarrassed, ashamed, tender): It's all right. Get up. Are you really crying? Or is it another trick, a few tears so I'll relent? Take that mask off, take it off, I want to see the seductive lie on your face.
No! Stop! Wait a moment!

(He runs to the door, cracks open the peep-hole, looks outside and comes back.)

Now take off the mask.

(Stella takes off her mask, revealing a charming and desolate face. Bruno, struck, lets out a cry of tenderness and compassion.)

Oh! A miracle! How sad and lovely your eyes are! Stella, for pity's sake, no more tears, forgive me! My dove, my snowdrop, my delicate flame! Like a little bird under its mother's wing, so my heart is beneath your gaze!
Don't cry. Get up or I'll throw myself to the ground, worm that I am.

(He slips down onto his knees in front of where she is kneeling.)

You were hot under the mask! Let me at least wipe the dew from your brow, my poor beloved.

It's the mask that does this to me. You will never wear it again! I think it was Estrugo who convinced me to dress you up like that.

Oh! Let them admire you, let them desire you! All the better! Stella, your lips are swollen with youth, they melt like tropical fruits. Oh!... If you still can, adorable girl, forgive me!

STELLA: Oh, please be quiet! Everything about you is precious to me, your jealousy and your harshness as much as your sweetest raptures! Would my love be true if I refused to obey your wishes?

(They embrace.)

BRUNO: Estrugo is finished here! To hell with him, the kill-joy! *He* feeds my suspicions. Finished! Stella, why does he hate you so much?

(Baby talk.) Oh! Stellina! Snake charmer! Tame the vipers around me, sleep will come!...

STELLA *(hugging him)*: Oh! Yes! Sleep, with his seven league boots, flying to come warm his St'amata's colden heart?

BRUNO *(joyous, exalted)*: Take off that cape! Let trust be reborn! The tears of Saint Lawrence in my soul! Rain! Rain down your stars, heavenly, until morning! If Estrugo comes back, I'll kill him, I'll slay him! How he must have envied our happiness. Solitude has shriveled him up. Let him go eat locusts in the desert.

STELLA *(with a little laugh)*: Locusts! And scorpions!

BRUNO: How could I have been so cruel? Get rid of that black cloak. I'll buy you a dress trimmed with lace, and golden slippers, and spidery silk stockings. A fine straw hat. Each morning you'll pick fresh flowers for your hat. And we'll strut up and down in the town square!

STELLA *(happily)*: Me with a filigree necklace and you with a red tie, twirling an iron-tipped cane.

(A knock on the door.)

BRUNO (quickly, worried): Hush! (He gets up.) Did somebody knock? Get up!

STELLA (imploring): Oh, no! Not again!

BRUNO (in a low voice): If it's Estrugo, he's finished! Definitely finished. Get up.

STELLA: Alas! Alas!

(He reaches his hands to her, helps her get up.)

BRUNO (pulling her towards him): Let him wait!

I'll give you a pink dress as well, with three ruffles, and another dress, blue, with wide pleats, and another dress, violet and fitted!

(Another knock.)

Shh! It's him, it's Estrugo, I'll reprimand him at once. He must be crazy, making up these twisted stories...
Put your cloak back on all the same. Someone might be spying on us through the cracks in the doors, if there are any cracks...

STELLA (smiles sadly): My cloak? Over my dress with the three ruffles...

BRUNO (uneasy): Later, the dress later... Hurry... Now! Now! Put your—Now!—put your mask back on too, for the last time... Now! You refuse?

STELLA (quickly): Oh! No, my love. I am ugly.

BRUNO (looks at her with the mask on and the hood pulled forward): It's Estrugo's work, yes... He taunts me, he's lost his reason. Oh! I'll tell him, make no mistake... Go to your room.

(Another knock, louder this time.)

Hurry! No, wait. You really didn't leave last night? You really were crying before? You weren't making fun of me? Go to your room.

(She lowers her head and goes. He stops her again. Darkly:)

Don't work on your embroidery, it's maddening. I don't know what you see in those flowers, I don't know what visions you put into them. It's the kind of work that lets the imagination run wild.

(Knocking, twice as hard as before.)

Go to your room!

(She goes.)

(He opens the door to the street.)

(In front of ESTRUGO a YOUNG MAN comes in, very shy and ingenuous.)

What is it? Come in... come in... How can I help you? Yes, the shutters are closed, because of the heat, but you'll be able to see as soon as your eyes get used to the dark.

Come in, Estrugo... *(He takes ESTRUGO by the arm.)* Dear man, are you sure that it wasn't spite or jealousy that made you denounce Stella? Yes. Yes. *(To the YOUNG MAN.)* Have a seat, over there... *(To ESTRUGO.)* I beg you, dig deep into your thoughts, examine your conscience closely, replay in your mind the strange reports you brought... yes, I urge you to think. And if you can honestly say you have no ulterior motive, consider the facts yet again before you take a position. *(To the YOUNG MAN.)* What can I do for you? *(To ESTRUGO.)* Think how terrible it would be to accuse Stella wrongly... Of course, I trust the purity of your intentions, and yet, and yet...

Weigh, measure, examine, evaluate? And judge! Good old Estrugo!

(Pats him on the shoulder.)

(To the YOUNG MAN:)

Are you here for a love letter?

YOUNG MAN: Yes, please.

BRUNO *(dryly)*: That will be twenty sous! *(He laughs unpleasantly.)* Ha! Ha! They're all the same! Idiot!

What do you do in life, other than make love? You're not from around here?

YOUNG MAN: ...from Oostkerque. I'm a barrel-maker.

55

BRUNO: And you fill your barrels with tears.

YOUNG MAN: I do...

(He lowers his head and cries.)

BRUNO: You've come all the way from Oostkerque for some flowery turns of phrase! Ha! Ha! You're losing a half day's pay, wearing down the soles of your boots, and all for a woman! Have you ever seen a woman who's worth a pair of boots? You've seen women and no woman! At ease, boy, I'll write your letter.

YOUNG MAN: We've loved each other for a month. And she's already growing indifferent...

BRUNO: Of course!... Say no more, I understand. It's my business to understand. Write, Estrugo, write:

(He dictates:)

"Ungrateful Wretch (capitalize those words!) and tenderly beloved (no capitals!), when our fingers interlaced, and we pressed so tight against each other that we seemed made only of light and shade, then people watched us from their doors, envious and angry, feeling cheated by our happiness. Oh! How rich they feel now!"

(Stops.)

(He looks at the YOUNG MAN with scorn. The man thinks for a long time.)

YOUNG MAN *(concluding)*: That's right.

(Then he straightens up, exalted.)

What a poet! What a poet!

(But BRUNO's cold stare forces him to sit down.)

Sorry...

BRUNO *(dictates)*: "My dove, my snowdrop, my delicate lamp! Like a little bird under its mother's wing, so is my heart beneath your gaze! Your lips are swollen with youth and they melt like tropical fruits."

(Dictating, he grows elated. Doubtless believing that the YOUNG MAN wishes to interrupt, he says with fury:)

Silence!

YOUNG MAN *(mechanically)*: Sorry…

BRUNO: Write, Estrugo, write!
"Alas! Like an ungrateful guest, you're already leaving without looking back. But, beware! If you separate your soul from mine, if your thoughts are not the exact models of mine, I'll kill you!"

YOUNG MAN *(shocked)*: No…

BRUNO: "If you utter a single unfamiliar word, I'll kill you!"

YOUNG MAN: No, no!

BRUNO: "…If you look at yourself three times in the mirror without laughing, if you smooth out your skirt for no reason…"

(He is under the influence of some particular agitation.)

I'll kill her! I'll kill her tonight on the slightest proof of her treachery! My shotgun is fully loaded.

(This time even ESTRUGO stands up, appalled. But BRUNO gets hold of himself and laughs, insofar as he is able.)

I don't mean it!… When inspiration takes hold, I sometimes stray from good sense. The storm clouds in my mind! One day my impulsive imagination will take over.
Calm yourself.
It's true, sometimes dream blurs so much with reality that I can no longer separate them… Where were we? Write, Estrugo!
Dear sir, give me some more details so I can finish. Is your sweetheart also from Oostkerque?

YOUNG MAN: Oh, no, she lives here: in the village!

BRUNO: You don't say? Then I must know her. I won't ask her name—we're famous for our discretion. She is beautiful.

YOUNG MAN: The most beautiful woman for miles around.

BRUNO *(blanches)*: The most beautiful woman? For miles around? You said the most beautiful? Estrugo, do you hear? The most beautiful, you say? You're sure?

YOUNG MAN: Everyone says so.

BRUNO *(Suddenly furious, he shakes the terrified YOUNG MAN.)*: And you're not afraid to admit it, you don't tremble to say that! Estrugo! You dare to look us in the face! *The most beautiful* woman, Estrugo, we know who that is!

(Again he regains control of himself.)

Ah! There, forgive me, dear man. Another fit of lyricism. I take such an interest in your case... You're a sly one, Estrugo.
The most beautiful woman! Ha! Ha! Ha!
You don't know Stella, no, no, you don't know her in all her beauty, eh? She's a thyrsus, a caduceus, a torch of living alabaster, a cluster of grapes, a ripening orchard!
Her skin is warm and delicious, she has a beauty mark...

YOUNG MAN: Above her knee...

BRUNO: High, delicate breasts...

YOUNG MAN: ...a birthmark...

BRUNO *(faltering)*: How do you know that?

YOUNG MAN: Everyone knows it.

BRUNO *(moves away and sighs)*: Bury me now!
No, no, be quiet, don't call out! It's just dizziness... Estrugo, I can see light breaking! You are a hypocrite! Stay mute, it makes no difference now... Oh! My heart!

(To the YOUNG MAN.)

You see, I'm sick, a little sick... Estrugo don't abandon me. I need to get some air... But don't worry, you haven't come all this way for nothing. Wait for me, I'll take care of the letter when I return.

(He gets up with difficulty.)

My wife will keep you company.

(He goes towards the door.)

Estrugo, the light will break through... *(He calls out.)* Stella! Stella! Dear heart! Yes, come here. Take off that cloak. Yes, I permit it. Take that mask off, too. She's playing at dressing up, young man. *(To Stella.)* Get on with it!

STELLA *(deeply astonished, without mask or cloak)*: Here I am, my love.

BRUNO *(to ESTRUGO)*: What powers of dissimulation! They don't even flinch! —No, I didn't say anything.
Dear heart, keep this young man company while I'm away. I need to get some air. I'll go as far as the castle, since I have business there anyway. That will give me a good walk... You keep the young man company... I'll be back in half an hour.

(To the YOUNG MAN, with a tight smile.)

You won't be bored with her company, I trust. Come, Estrugo, come. Half an hour, neither more nor less, you can count the minutes... Come, Estrugo... The seconds....

(They leave, closing the door.)

(Silent scene.)

(STELLA and the MAN FROM OOSTKERQUE remain motionless. No gesture, no look.)

(Two statues.)

(Long silence.)

(BRUNO appears at the second-floor window, spying on them. Now all three are immobile. Prolonged silence.)

BRUNO *(exclaims at last)*: Out of my mind, I've been out of my mind!

(Two cries of fright. BRUNO gesticulates.)

My trap, rendered toothless by their restraint! Cooper, I'll break you like a barrel-stave! Villains! They won't move a hair, knowing I lie in wait. Oh! If only I'd surprised them! Your silence gives you away! That stiffness is as good as an embrace.

Estrugo, stop him! I want to scrape the skin from his bones!

(He disappears.)

(ESTRUGO enters, terrified, loquacious.)

ESTRUGO: Young man, run, save yourself! I think Bruno's been hit in the head!

STELLA *(trembling)*: Oh God!

ESTRUGO: In one of these fits he's capable of anything! Your letter? Oh! You see what love is? Better not to write, and if possible hold your tongue!

(The YOUNG MAN disappears).

BRUNO *(cries from outside)*: Oh! Traitor! You're young enough to run! Fly, fly, I'll hunt you down, I'll have my revenge! Too young—you're taking the quickest path to perdition!

(And BRUNO comes back, lighthearted, extraordinarily so.)

STELLA *(nonplussed)*: My dearest love, was that really you?

BRUNO *(laughs)*: Really me? Will you confess, then?

STELLA *(smiling, relieved)*: What could I confess that you don't already know?

BRUNO *(ambivalently)*: Do you hear that, Estrugo? Her answers always have two meanings; one soothes, the other poisons... Oh! Oh!...
Estrugo, you love me, please go straight to Petrus. Beg him not to leave before we've reconciled. He's leaving next week, you know. Shower him with honeyed words: say I'm not strong enough to go to him myself and tell him that

shame holds me back. I was harsh with him. But now I can compensate him for my bad behavior. Tell him that. And say that, if he has any memory of our former affection, he should come at once. Go, go. I swear, Estrugo, I await him with humility. Bring him here.

(He pushes ESTRUGO out the door.)

STELLA *(moved)*: Oh! Bruno, am I to hope or fear?

BRUNO *(too gaily)*: Oh! Stella!... First let's open the doors and windows... *(He opens them wide.)* And the shutters! Let anyone who desires you see you in all your glory! The reign of darkness is over, the light will break through. What? Estrugo. It's true, he's gone.

STELLA *(still incredulous)*: Is it possible?

BRUNO *(contemplates her and smiles)*: And your beauty will dazzle me as well. From now on, you can come and go as you like, I'm not going to shut you away anymore. What good can come of such strictness?

STELLA *(mad with joy)*: He's cured! My dearly beloved, miraculously cured!

BRUNO: Not yet, but you can cure me. If you want to?

STELLA *(taking him in her arms)*: Oh, now, now!

(He sits down and takes her on his lap.)

BRUNO: Listen to me with both ears. I've aged quite a bit in the past three months. My complexion is bad, I choke with bile, nightmares give me cramps, my hair's falling out!... If I keep worrying like this, I'll die.

STELLA: Oh! Don't talk like that!... I'll make it better. Tell me the cure.

BRUNO: I will... I count your every footstep throughout the house; I follow your gaze to see if it escapes the walls of your room; I number your sighs; I watch over your restless sleep; I imprison your body; but is there a way to imprison your thoughts?
Stella, let's talk like grown-ups.
I'm not waiting for you to confess, I know your lips are sealed.

Ssh! Listen to me.

A husband, however cunning, will never figure out his wife's tricks, however stupid she may be. And you have ingenuity to spare!

So, I'll give up hoarding my treasure.

But my perpetual state of doubt exhausts and weakens me. The inflammation chiefly afflicts my liver. I don't want to doubt any longer, do you understand? This doubt, this oppressive doubt—I will fight and destroy it today.

STELLA: Thank God!

BRUNO: Yes, and the Devil too…. You see, I know the cure for this doubt, the absolute, immediate cure, the universal panacea. In order for me not to doubt your faithfulness, I must know that you are unfaithful!

STELLA *(shocked)*: What?

BRUNO *(in sudden fury)*: I must know that you are unfaithful!

(He quickly calms down and tries to reassure her).

Don't worry. I know what I'm doing. Stay here. I told you. Since you meet my doubt with silence, I will do this to obtain proof of your degeneracy. You will betray me under my own roof, today, in my very presence.

STELLA *(in consternation, backing away from him)*: My love, what are you saying?

BRUNO *(simply)*: Then you want me to die?

STELLA: Oh, oh! Never. But at least I can die. Kill me.

BRUNO *(in a lively tone)*: Not before you reveal your secret! Maybe after.
There's no other solution. Either I am a cuckold or I die. It's inevitable that a husband will be betrayed, and that's exactly what I want. There's no other way. Ridicule and suffering are the offspring of ignorance and doubt. I will be the first to learn of my shame.

STELLA: My love, take pity on me. Remember that I was pure when you first knew me. I didn't even know what things were called… I am as innocent now, because love erases sin…

BRUNO: Exactly! I want you to be impure and me to be dishonored.

There's no compromise. I'll be a cuckold today or a corpse. It's the horns or the rope. You choose.

STELLA (trembling): I wouldn't have the courage to...! Another man...that would be awful. Bruno, you're joking, aren't you? Is this some kind of test? Even the thought makes me shrivel...

BRUNO (impassively): Choose for me. Will it be the horns or will it be the rope?

STELLA: What more can this man do to me? Bruno, I'd rather lie to you...I'll confess whatever it is you want. If anyone comes near me, I'll bite him. Please, you're scaring me.

BRUNO: Choose for me, Stella.

STELLA: After, you won't be able to look at me. And as for me?... People will point at me!... I love you enough to die for you, but...

BRUNO: It is braver to suffer a long time than to die in an instant.

STELLA: ...and enough to suffer, too, Bruno, but...

BRUNO: It shouldn't be so hard for you!

STELLA: Oh! But it is! It is!

BRUNO (explodes): Argh! Enough of this! Choose!

STELLA: Please!...

BRUNO: Choose...

(Pause.)

STELLA (in tears): I'll obey... You are my master... I'll obey... But you must know how much love it takes for me to betray you.

BRUNO (with a sort of ardent calm): Very good. I've summoned Petrus.

STELLA (cries out): Oh, no! With him!

BRUNO: Don't protest, don't cry, or I'll think it's not for my sake that you're so careful of your virtue. That's a lot of noise to make just for a husband!...

STELLA *(sighing)*: With Petrus!

BRUNO *(after a short pause, gently)*: Yes. I humiliated Petrus and I owe him recompense. I can give it to him no more fully.

STELLA: Thankfully, he won't agree.

BRUNO: *(in a peremptory tone)*. He'll agree, I hope. So it's settled, I'll be relieved of this crushing doubt. Once a cuckold, I can act like a cuckold.

STELLA: Will I be able to go on living?

BRUNO: Perhaps. Who knows. I can't be sure how I'll be. I know doubt but not certitude. We'll see. Knowing is all.

STELLA *(her arms around BRUNO's neck)*: Oh! Cruel man, why must I love you?

BRUNO *(quickly)*: Watch out, here's Petrus. If he refuses, help me insist.

STELLA *(in a low voice, quickly)*: Please reconsider...

BRUNO: Now's the time, now's the time!

STELLA: You won't be any happier after.

BRUNO: I will, I will, be sure of that...

STELLA: And me?

BRUNO: You live for me.

STELLA: But...

BRUNO: Quiet.

(ESTRUGO shows in PETRUS.)

Estrugo, leave us. Don't go far from the door, I'll call you.

(PETRUS walks towards BRUNO and with great ease offers him his hand.)

PETRUS: Hello, Bruno.

BRUNO *(triumphantly to STELLA)*: He'll accept!

PETRUS: Hello, little cousin.

(STELLA lowers her eyes and blushes.)

Don't be ashamed, Stella, all is forgotten.

BRUNO: Really? Thank you, Petrus, thank you. You have a generous heart. I always knew it. He'll accept, Stella! I'm saved!

PETRUS: I wouldn't have been able to leave without seeing you two again. I'd have come back on my own…

BRUNO: Look how magnanimous he is! I wasn't in my right mind that day…. Don't look at me so intently… I appear disturbed to you, don't I?

PETRUS: Yes, you do. Are you sick?

BRUNO *(smiles crookedly)*: A peculiar malady, which grips my every part.

PETRUS: Why didn't you call me?

BRUNO: It's not too late, if you offer me the comfort I need.

STELLA *(murmers)*: Please…

BRUNO: That day, that day, Petrus, when you looked at Stella—with my consent—your eyes were like two glowing embers.

PETRUS: Let's not discuss it anymore.

BRUNO: To the contrary!

(He quickens.)

Since then, jealously has twisted, grilled, lacerated me. I haven't had a moment's peace. Stella's every gesture, her every word, each beat of her heart, her silence, her immobility, whether she's awake or asleep, everything that she is in time and in space is cause for anguish! I am jealous with a fury that is destroying me. Doubt courses through me, madly following a thousand trails that hold her scent. Tally ho! Tally ho! Petrus, it must be pushed to its limit.

STELLA *(in a half voice)*: Please…

BRUNO: Be quiet!

(He is exalted.)

Doubt either kills me or I kill it! Regarding a wife's fidelity, one can only guess. There's no absolute proof of her infidelity. Hans Carvel with the devil's ring only slips a finger into certainty. While Mrs. Carvel sleeps, her mind does not. Even the devil could be made a cuckold. What's the use of surveillance?

STELLA: Please…

BRUNO *(furious)*: Silence, Mrs. Carvel!

Here, the body will guide the mind and all will be consumed! To be overcome by doubt or to overcome it! Only proof of the crime can save me, monstrous though it may be. I require proof.

(He grows even more excited.)

Petrus, grant me the certitude that will save me.

PETRUS: *(shocked)*. What?

BRUNO: *(banging the table with his fists)*. To compensate you for the injury I did to you, Petrus, injure me in return. Take Stella, and let the devil protest. Take her; I give her to you. She's ready. Now lead her to her bedroom. I consent, invite, ask, implore you.

(He cries out.)

I beg you on my knees!

(Panting.)

She'll go with you, she's prepared... Go up together, shut yourselves in, torturers! Let sparks fly from your bodies as from two stones struck together. Kill me with your flame! And plant horns on my forehead so large they cast a shadow over the land...

(He is exhausted.)

What will I do? I'll kill her, I'll chase her out, I'll pardon her, I don't know, but I will have acted.

PETRUS *(bursts out in wild laughter and sits down, his hands by his sides)*: This is fantastic!... I can't stop laughing. He's completely crazy!

BRUNO *(pale)*: Coward! Coward!

PETRUS *(stands up, also pale)*: Bruno!

BRUNO: Poltroon!

STELLA *(terrified, coming between them)*: Oh! Petrus, have pity on us. You can see he's very ill.

BRUNO: Weakling! Weakling!

PETRUS *(trying to leave)*: Good bye.

STELLA *(holding him back)*: Petrus, don't leave me with him like this. If you ever loved him as I love him, don't go!

BRUNO *(with an insulting laugh)*: He'll leave you holding onto his gold braid...

PETRUS *(stops; in a menacing tone)*: Watch it, Bruno.

BRUNO: My dear, you're not hot enough for him. He likes spicy food. You're only good to a tired tongue like mine.

STELLA *(grabbing PETRUS)*: Petrus, we must help him. Don't push me away now that I've abandoned my modesty. Cousin, don't insult my despair.

BRUNO: Find flies to sting him with!... The rose bush is swarming with them. Shake the bush, Stella, shake it!

PETRUS (*intently*): Watch out, Bruno. I might take you at your word!

BRUNO: You wouldn't dare.

PETRUS (*rising*): I won't be made a fool of!

BRUNO: You wouldn't dare, my captain!

PETRUS (*with a glacial energy*): Come, Stella.

BRUNO (*a cry of joy*): Ah!

PETRUS: Be a cuckold, if that's what you want!

(*He walks quickly across the room, followed by STELLA in a state of resignation.*)

STELLA: God forgive me for loving so much...

BRUNO (*exultant*): Go, Stella, go, Petrus; onward, warriors!

PETRUS (*on the stairs*): Come on, cousin.

BRUNO: And make sure you lock the door!... And even if I bang on the door and yell, you must stay entwined like a pair of initials. This is what I want.

PETRUS: (*going into the bedroom*): Come, Stella! We'll do what he wants!

STELLA (*to BRUNO*): I'm the unhappiest woman alive.

BRUNO: Go on, good little slut!

(*They shut the door.*)

(*BRUNO, exhausted, collapses onto the couch.*)

(*Long silence.*)

(*Then, BRUNO calls out in a broken voice:*)

Estrugo! Estrugo!

(*Silence.*)

(*ESTRUGO comes in alarmed.*)

ESTRUGO: You're as pale as a lamp in daylight!

BRUNO (*stupified*): Estrugo, I believe we're on the verge of a disaster... And all because of my eloquence. My fervor!

Creep upstairs on tiptoe. Do as I say! Something disturbing is happening. Shh, not a sound!...

(ESTRUGO goes upstairs. BRUNO doesn't turn around.)

Take care not to make the floor creak. Are you there yet? Look through the keyhole... *(Aside.)* Very disturbing. Very disturbing.

(ESTRUGO puts his eye to the keyhole. He draws back, speechless, and gestures for BRUNO's attention.)

BRUNO *(very calm)*: Well?

(ESTRUGO comes down quickly and stops in front of BRUNO. Gestures speechlessly; he is choked up.)

What is it?

ESTRUGO *(his speech suddenly released)*: Petrus with Stella, Stella with Petrus, Petrus with Stella, shut up in the bedroom!

BRUNO *(simply)*: No.

ESTRUGO *(with astonishing volubility)*: Gold braid and sails, I swear it, the curtains are drawn. Petrus and Stella, I swear, shut up in there together.

BRUNO *(stubborn)*: No, no.

ESTRUGO *(slightly slower)*: Look in my eyes, the picture might still be there. I saw them!

BRUNO *(suddenly stands up in front of him and yells with fury)*: You're lying! You're lying!

ESTRUGO *(trembling but firm)*: Stellus and Petra!

BRUNO *(crazed)*: You're lying a hundred times over.

(ESTRUGO is again reduced to gestures. BRUNO hurriedly takes down his shotgun.)

(ESTRUGO, terrified, runs away shouting:)

ESTRUGO: Help! Help! Murder! Murder!

BRUNO *(in a fury)*: Idiot! You think I'm aiming at you?

(He's too late. ESTRUGO has disappeared.)

(BRUNO's fury increases.)

I'll kill them, I'll slaughter them both! As soon as they come out, they're dead. I'll spit on their carcasses.

(He calls out ferociously.)

Stella! Petrus! Open the door so I can strike you down. Like dogs in at the kill. Kill! Kill! Petrus, you must die! Stella, you'll be caught on the Devil's pitchfork! Come down!

(He rushes up the stairs.)

Fornicators! Into the fiery furnace with them! Let harpies suck out their marrow. Petrus, there's a man here waiting for you.

(He bangs the stock of his gun on the door.)

Why not confess, you devils? Haven't you had enough? You dare defy me under my own roof? Open the door, Stella!

(His fury ends in frenetic despair.)

I knew I'd be weak, I told them to pay no attention to my pleading. Stella, disobey me just this one little time! Ah! This is extreme cruelty; I am keeping the door shut against me.

(He kneels.)

Have pity! I want to be a cuckold but not so much of one! Please come out! My fury has gone miraculously! There's no need to go any further. Petrus, you're a brave captain, it's been proven! Stella, I feel cuckold enough!

(Silence. He stands up, somber, resolved. He goes downstairs.)

Then I'll kill them. Their souls are lost, and so is mine.

(Sounds of a crowd outside.)

VOICES: This way, everyone! This way, officers! Be careful! No shooting unless I say so. Some discipline here! He's crazy! Everyone together now! Forward!

(The crowd bursts into the house. Town police, led by the MAYOR. ESTRUGO follows, cautiously.)

MAYOR: Halt! Don't move!

BRUNO *(seeing ESTRUGO)*: Idiot! What's all this noise?

MAYOR: Officers! Hold him!

BRUNO *(argues, outraged)*: Am I not master here? My friends, you have nothing to fear. I'm being defied, I'm being mocked, I'm being wounded to the heart. I have the right. My beloved wife Stella, my wife, is up there, shut in the bedroom with her cousin Petrus. Ah! Estrugo, didn't you see them? *(Answering for him.)* Yes, he says. Through the keyhole. Her and him.

MAYOR *(outraged)*: Stella!

ESTRUGO: With Petrus: Petrus and Stella!

BRUNO: Soiling my sheets, if you will. Justice! Let go of me! I'll kill them!

MAYOR: Bruno, the law is on your side. No judge in the world would condemn you, not if he has a wife...

BRUNO: Bravo! Free me!

MAYOR: Well then, kill Stella if you want, but I can't help you do it. Of course I can't, she hasn't betrayed me.

BRUNO *(strident)*: Not yet, but just wait...

MAYOR *(simply)*: Perhaps. But you should have avoided this scene.

BRUNO: Ah! Estrugo, you traitor! It's always you who destroys me.

MAYOR *(in a low voice)*: Shh! I hear the lock turning up there.

BRUNO *(also in a low voice)*: Let me go.

MAYOR *(forcefully)*: Hold him tight. Somebody's turning the key.

(Silence. Intense curiosity. BRUNO is held fast.)

(The upstairs door opens.)

(PETRUS and STELLA appear.)

STELLA *(terrified)*: Oh! My love, what are all these people doing here?

(She comes down reluctantly.)

PETRUS *(laughing gaily)*: There, Bruno, you got what you asked for and more.

BRUNO *(slowly)*: Is this true, Stella?

STELLA *(reddening)*: From now on you can be happy...

(BRUNO and the crowd look at the young man and woman.)

PETRUS *(bowing gracefully to STELLA)*: Goodbye, Stella. Goodbye, little cousin. No doubt we won't see each other again. When I ship out, I'll take with me a precious memory and a potent regret. Your image will haunt me. Please forgive me if I've harmed you in any way.

(He tries to kiss her hand, she quickly snatches it back.)

STELLA *(ashamed)*: Oh no, not that!

(Suddenly, to everyone's astonishment, BRUNO bursts out laughing.)

BRUNO: Ha! Ha! What a farce! They want to trick me! Friends, hang up my gun. My dear Petrus, I'm subtler than you are. *(To the MAYOR.)* He blackens himself to scare me, don't you understand? Ha! Ha! The two of them together came up with this shabby trick. No, no, they can't fool me! I don't believe any of it!

PETRUS *(shrugs his shoulders and goes out)*: Farewell. I don't want to ruin you, but you're as foolish as a man could be. Farewell.

BRUNO: Goodbye, my excellent Petrus, don't hold anything against me. I'll come to see you off.

STELLA *(in despair)*: Bruno, was my sacrifice for nothing?

BRUNO *(laughs, and the whole crowd with him)*: Come closer to me, naughty girl. *(He presses her to him.)* She thinks I'm that naïve! Ha! Ha! You don't know how to lie.

ESTRUGO *(springing up, indignant)*: Bruno, I saw them through the keyhole, saw them and saw them again!

BRUNO *(with a gentle slap)*: Yes, thank you very much. I know you're my devoted friend! That's enough!

(To the crowd.)

Go home, my friends, go home in peace, you're all honest lads. I'm trusting you with Stella. She's in your care and in Petrus's care; they deserve each other.

(The crowd goes out, laughing.)

STELLA *(fearful)*: Bruno, are you completely cured?

BRUNO: Yes!

(But he has a look of pain on his face.)

Estrugo, the pain reawakes. If it's not Petrus, then who is it?

CURTAIN

ACT THREE

(The same set.

The windows are wide open, showing the September countryside. It is late afternoon. STELLA, in the orchard, is laughing very loudly, surrounded by a group of young men.

Inside, BRUNO, looking older and broken-down, faces a line of young men sitting, like children, on the ground against the wall.

He is writing. Long silence.

ESTRUGO enters, his movements tormented and rapid.

He goes to BRUNO and whispers in his ear. BRUNO listens calmly. The audience doesn't hear what ESTRUGO says.

But BRUNO responds, laughing:)

BRUNO: Child's play! Child's play!

(ESTRUGO goes on speaking in a low voice.)

Oh, no! Don't believe your eyes, dear man!

(ESTRUGO gestures towards the window as if to say: "See for yourself." BRUNO doesn't turn his head. He laughs.)

Ha! Ha! That? You're naïve as ever. What do you see exactly? If Stella wanted to misbehave, wouldn't she be more secretive? You're judging by appearances. Poor man, she'll dupe you completely!

(Because ESTRUGO continues to protest and gesticulate, BRUNO rouses himself somewhat.)

That's enough! I'm telling you, you won't upset me. She's faking, she's playing with those milksops, those mooncalves—the same way she played with Petrus: to beguile my rightful vigilance.

STELLA *(outside, pursued by the horde of lovers)*: Bruno! Bruno, help! They're making me! Four of them! My dear husband, help me!

(She's laughing very loudly.)

BRUNO *(also laughing, shouts)*: Tell them to be patient, my kitten! Everyone gets a turn!

(The young men in the house begin to punch one another with masculine glee.)

VOICES: You and me! Me and you! Everyone gets a turn! Everyone gets some! Unless he's a mule...

BRUNO (*after a stunned moment, smiles and winks*): Child's play!

(*He gets up. Cheerful.*)

And I'm all through here!

(*Uproar. The YOUNG MEN surround him.*)

VOICES: Here! Me first! Why? Everyone gets a turn!

BRUNO (*playfully pushing them back*): Troublemakers! Now: the letters are all written in the same style. Each is exactly thirty lines long, full of lyrical phrases: a real rhapsody! You can have one for twenty sous. You don't get to choose, you blockheads! Any of them will touch your beloved's heart. It doesn't matter which you take.

(*He laughs heartily.*)

Ha! Ha! Love is one hell of a joke!

(*The YOUNG MEN pay, each takes his letter and they exit tumultuously.*)

VOICES: Good bye... It's my turn to play... Yes, the game's in the square. Good bye! Get the dice! Get the coins! Get the balls!

(*They leave amid shouts of laughter.*)

(*BRUNO takes ESTRUGO by the arm.*)

BRUNO (*smiling with good cheer*): I'm telling you, you shouldn't be too hasty. Stella's whole game—which disgusts you—is only an act to confuse me, a trap she's laying for me. But don't worry, I won't fall in. Stella only shows us what will prove her decency. *She pretends.*

ESTRUGO (*after forceful gestures*): But Bruno, I swear I saw that ugly blacksmith kiss her on the mouth!

BRUNO (*laughing*): Are you trying to confuse me? Ha! You'll have to try harder than that!... It's perfectly possible that he kissed her, and others before and others after. What does it matter? Am I a lark to be lured by a glittering mirror? She's *seeming* to obey me! I told her, "I won't be satisfied until all the men of the village between the ages of fifteen and sixty have visited your bedroom!" Ha! Ha! This is a new strategy! She makes a show of obedience, so I let her alone and don't ask too many questions. But I am determined to know!

ESTRUGO: Doesn't she shut herself in with at least one of them a day?

BRUNO *(triumphant)*: Oh! What innocence! What prodigious naïveté! *They pretend!* I'm telling you! The truth is never straightforward. Is it conceivable that a young woman of good breeding would act with such depravity, in broad daylight, right under her husband's nose? You've lost your mind! Is it possible that her husband, who is so deeply in love with her—because I am desperately, horribly in love, Estrugo!—would tolerate such unheard-of degeneracy? Who would believe that and how could you, you innocent, believe it?

ESTRUGO: There are already a hundred bragging that they've had her just the way they wanted. And look at you: you're plucked, dried up, broken down, as though you were the hero in all their stories!

BRUNO: It's normal to boast at their age.

ESTRUGO: For pity's sake! What will it take?

BRUNO *(with a wicked joy)*: What I need to find out from all the men who come here is who *doesn't* come. The one who doesn't court her—he's the man she hopes to save from my vengeance. She hides her malice with exaggerated good humor, with evasions, detours, convolutions. And I pretend as much as she does. But the one she cherishes secretly *(he stumbles)*—nothing, nothing, a little dizziness, that's all—she won't welcome that one with me watching...be sure of that. It will be a bad day for the man who doesn't show up.

ESTRUGO: But what if he did come?

BRUNO: He won't come, you ass *(He laughs again.)* And even then... I have a plan. Tonight we'll find out whether she's really betraying us—of her own will!

(STELLA rushes into the room, laughing madly. Her suitors pull her around and kiss her. Among them we see the YOUNG MEN whose letters BRUNO was writing.)

STELLA *(gleefully defending herself)*: Let me go, you rascals! Bruno, save me!

VOICES: Her neck! Here, Stella! Choose! Her little breast is cold!

STELLA: No poaching! Ha! Help, Bruno.

VOICES: Choose, or I'll take you without asking! She's got nothing on under her dress!

STELLA *(hiding in BRUNO's arms)*: Bruno! They've messed up my hair, they've made me black and blue!... They've ravaged me!

BRUNO (*amiably, to the YOUNG MEN, who have paused*): There, there, calm down!... He who plucks the flowers never tastes the fruit! Stop shouting, stop waving your arms, my friends! Look at Stella: she may seem forward, but she's delicate, she's frail. Be gentle. In order to share her, you've got to keep her intact. Ha! Ha! That's the miracle of it...

VOICES: Bravo! Ha! Ha! Long live Bruno!

STELLA (*sweetly*): My love, please ask them not to insist so much. Their hands are cold and their beards scratch.

BRUNO: Did you hear that?

ALL (*with clamorous enthusiasm*): We did!!!

BRUNO: Treat her as she deserves. She is fresh, unstained, barely hatched. (*To STELLA.*) Go on, my soul, go on. (*To the YOUNG MEN.*) I give her to you, but be gentle... (*To STELLA.*) Go on, go on. (*She is immediately taken, snatched up by the group of greedy YOUNG MEN.*)

SHOUTS: Come here! Hands off! Long live Bruno! Let's divide her up!

STELLA (*cries out loudly*): You, you'll be punished. Oh! He pinched me! You can fight all you want, but let me go! You, your day will never come!...

VOICES: But my night will! She's fatter than Jeannette. Read my letter! No, mine! —And whiter, too. —She blows hot and cold, depending.

BRUNO (*to ESTRUGO*): What's that look on your face? Don't believe everything you see, Estrugo, don't believe everything you see.

(*The HERDSMAN enters. He sees BRUNO laughing and STELLA defending herself from the group.*)

HERDSMAN (*furious*): Marcel, you pig! John! Jacob! Quentin! You mongrels! Stop! Bruno, Bruno, I spit on you.

(*He leaps forward into the crowd and violently pushes the young men back.*)

Get back, Arthus, that's enough. The rest of you, I'll fix you so you can't walk straight!

MAN (*advancing towards the HERDSMAN*): Well, you'll get as good as you give, you toad.

VOICES: Hit him! Hit him!

(*But STELLA is already between them, and BRUNO leaps forward.*)

'Page 56

(Quick movements. The dialogue is like whiplash.)

STELLA *(to the HERDSMAN)*: Do you dare?

BRUNO: Maniac!

HERDSMAN: I spit on you!

ALL: Hit him! Hit him!

STELLA: Shut up!

BRUNO: What do you want?

STELLA *(standing between the group, which advances menacingly, and the HERDSMAN, who is backing away)*: Be quiet, all of you! Are you really my master or are you just trying to make them think so?

ALL: Throw him in the manure pit!

BRUNO: Yes? Are you her master?

STELLA: Can't I do what I want with my body, if Bruno lets me? What right do you have?

HERDSMAN: I'll crush them!

ALL: Oh! Scary!

STELLA: You have the right to claim your turn, no more and no less.

HERDSMAN: I don't share with swine!

CLAMOR: Ha! Ha! He's been neutered! Show us, if you're all there! ...

BRUNO *(leaps forward)*: You'll share, my fighting cock, or I'll shave your spurs. You'll take your turn like the others. Let the one who doesn't show up beware.

STELLA *(quickly, frightened)*: Bruno, don't get carried away! If he doesn't come, I'll go to him. Calm down.

ALL: Let everyone see: he's a eunuch! A soprano!

BRUNO: Let the one who doesn't show up.

ALL: Kick him out! Beat him! Into the pit with him! Get him!

HERDSMAN *(still backing away)*: I'll be waiting outside to take you on one by one.

STELLA *(in front of the door)*: Leave and you lose your turn! *(To BRUNO.)*

He'll be back, my love, don't worry.

(The tumult is great. A fight is just about to break out when the MAYOR arrives with the TOWN GUARD. He has a shotgun on his shoulder and is followed by a crowd of WOMEN.)

MAYOR *(loudly, his voice strained)*: What a scandal! What a scandal! Bruno! Quiet! Stop! How long is this scandal going to go on?

(Astonished silence.)

HERDSMAN *(spitting on the ground)*: Go on, Bruno. I'm not sharing.

(Sensation.)

MAYOR *(yells)*: Nobody move! I'll arrest anyone who does.

(The HERDSMAN is gone.)

BRUNO *(jeering after him)*: Run away, Stella knows how to bring you back—if you're up to it...

(He laughs.)

MAYOR *(shocked, self-important)*: Oh! Bruno, what's the point of all this? Have I become your worst enemy? Are you trying to get me discharged? Are you discontent with the government of this county? Unhappy with my laws? — Silence, back there!

(The MAYOR changes his tone. Now he seems truly distressed.)

Bruno, can you be the same brave, intelligent boy I watched grow up? (You graduated from school at age twelve!) Stella, are you still the Stella whose modesty was an example to all?

STELLA *(laughs, maybe too loudly)*: Ha! Ha! *(To BRUNO.)* They can't understand the wonder of our love!

BRUNO: Let them talk, my blossom, and follow your heart.

MAYOR: Reconsider, my son... What's the good of rebelling against the custom of the country? You are—and Stella too—the disgrace of a loyal region. Decent people are ashamed to live near you.

BRUNO *(rubbing his hands)*: Excellent!

MAYOR: Our young men (they've got nothing but air between their ears) dream of Stella when they should be working. Their wives fear for the sanctity of their homes. In every village that gets wind of your strange perversions, the

authorities convene, measures are taken. There's even talk of forbidding heads of households from leaving their homes. Dear boy, it's practically a state of siege.

BRUNO *(overjoyed)*: So much the better!

MAYOR: Watch out, Bruno!

STELLA *(holding BRUNO close)*: Oh, my love, soon you'll have what you dreamed of.

MAYOR *(angrily)*: Really, it's intolerable. Fights are breaking out all over the place. The night is full of shouts and sobs. Outraged women are threatening to set fire to the house and throw Stella into the river.

WOMEN SHOUTING: Into the river with her!

(A wave of anger.)

MAYOR *(furious)*: Everyone out! Shrews, get out! Guards, do your duty!

(The GUARDS push the crowd out.)

SHOUTING: Stella! I'll rip the hair off your belly! Shear the she-goat! The witch!

MAYOR: Guard the doors!

BRUNO: Foolish creatures! How can they be so easily cast aside? Have *I* been abandoned? Stella loves me now with a passion that would burn down thirty towns.

SHOUTING *(from ouside, under the window)*: We'll tattoo a sow on her belly! It can be her emblem! Drag her to the river!

(The TOWN GUARDS chase the crowd away.)

(The NURSE, who has come in during the uproar, moves to protect STELLA.)

NURSE: What devils! Why can't they let a person be happy in her own way? Don't be scared, my little nymph, I'll protect you.... I can be fierce, you know! Come with me...

(She pulls STELLA away and they go out together.)

(The MAYOR sits down, out of breath.)

MAYOR: My goodness, what a struggle. Bruno, now that we're alone I want you to listen to me. Be careful. Today is the feast of Saint-Géraud, the patron saint of our town. You know this.

BRUNO (*very cheerful*): I do, and I have my plans.

MAYOR: Then know this too: our people also have plans. In an hour, it will be dark. Watch out! They want their revenge.

BRUNO: Yes, yes, in an hour!

MAYOR: Mascarades, serenades, other follies.

BRUNO (*full of lively contentment*): Quite so, quite so!

MAYOR. Something tells me you won't enjoy the farce. They plan to make you suffer.

BRUNO (*gaily*): Rest assured, I've got nothing to fear. You think other people are as credulous as you. Ha! Ha! You're a bit slow—no offense intended. These men don't come for Stella. They come for my services. All the rest is a delusion. I've never composed so many love letters in my life.

MAYOR: No offense intended, but you're dumber than a peeled frog. Never have I seen a man so blind. Those letters you write are all addressed to Stella!

BRUNO (*nastily*): Ha! What imagination! Whatever will they think of next? Mayor, your brain is muddled and your skull as flat as a monkey's ass. No offense intended, no offense intended!

MAYOR (*gets up, shocked*): To a magistrate!

(*He looks around uneasily. No one has heard. Relieved.*)

Mum's the word!

(*With great dignity:*) I'm warning you; I'll leave the mob for you to deal with.

Here's my last argument: It wouldn't be so bad if only men were concerned, but now the beasts are getting involved!

BRUNO: ???...

MAYOR: The beasts yes, the beasts! The birds are talking. Little children teach parrots and magpies phrases about you... Your tragic glory is complete. I had to issue a decree to restore order. I wrote it myself—I didn't dare ask for your help.

BRUNO (*sincerely shocked*): Why not?

MAYOR: You would have said no. I want you to know that your name is mentioned and that you are described and that the decree will be posted on the

Page 68

doors of the town hall and outside the hospital and the police station. I could read it to you.

BRUNO: Read, by all means read. You have our permission. Right? Estrugo?

MAYOR (*unfolding a piece of paper*): I was inspired by indignation.

"By order of the association of Mayors and Sheriffs, within a week all magpies, jays, crows, parrots and all other tame, speaking birds, to whom such phrases have been taught as, *Bruno is a cuckold, Whoever wants Bruno's wife...,* etcetera, will be confiscated.

"The officer charged with the confiscation will note in his register exactly what each bird knows how to say and in whose house it was found."

BRUNO (*darkening*): You're going to too much trouble, my good fellow. Really, you could have let the birds speak, we don't concern ourselves with that.

MAYOR (*furious*): Egotist! You think only of yourself! I will—for my own sake—establish order before the governor intervenes. Goodbye.

BRUNO (*laughing bitterly*): Summon the magpies and the crows. What will you call your tribunal?

MAYOR (*angrily*): And what will you call Stella's baby if she finds herself with child?

BRUNO (*grandly*): I'll call it Cortryk, after the village.

MAYOR (*defeated*): Keep on joking! I give up.

(*He goes.*)

(*BRUNO turns to ESTRUGO.*)

BRUNO (*recites*):

> Now as evening darkens
> already the feverish willow
> at the meadow's rim
> seizes the slender moon
> in its many arms!
> You will lose her, lose her!

(*He stops to complain.*)

Estrugo, I'm shamed more than the birds say.

I'd rather to be cuckolded a thousand and one times, as people think, than to be a cuckold once, as I am in fact. Stella is playing with all those wretches and with me (what does she tell them when she pulls them into her room?). You can be sure that up there she doesn't keep the promises she makes down here. You can see why they wouldn't boast of her strictness... I don't torture myself over this one or that one.

But the other one! Estrugo, the other one!

She protects the other one from my suspicions. He's the one she hides in the crowd, the one she receives in secret—(God knows when?)—the one who wounds me; in short, the other man, the one who escapes!

(He lowers his voice.)

When all the fools are gone and we're alone in the house, I track her every step, I scrutinize her, I sniff, I poke. I've found nothing yet. After she's dismissed another hare-brained dolt (pretending to be shameless...) I demand that she confess her treachery... I haven't gotten a thing out of her! Estrugo!

(He shakes himself and assumes a determined and jovial expression.)

Never mind! We'll be craftier than she is!

(He recites.)

> You will lose her, lose her!
> The frogs' golden eyes
> glisten like constellations
> at the edge of the pale ponds
> and with harsh notes they rejoice
> in their endless love-making.

(He laughs.)

I wrote that myself.

Estrugo, it's almost dusk now. Time to act. Follow me. We'll go to celebrate the saint—but in our own way. In one hour I'll prove to you that she's deceiving us.

(He calls out.)

Stella! Stella! My purest spring! Stella! You'll see I have nothing to fear from their farces. My own plan is clever enough.

(STELLA appears with the NURSE.)

NURSE: Have those devils left?

BRUNO: Stella, my sweet, bring me my coat and hat and my stick.

STELLA: Oh! My love, are you leaving me again?

BRUNO *(harshly)*: I must! Estrugo and I have a visit to pay. Isn't that right, old friend? *(After a delay, he answers himself.)* Yes, Bruno. —My hat, please.

NURSE: Stay here, dear child, let me go...

(She goes out.)

STELLA *(sighing)*: I'll be waiting..

BRUNO: You'll have plenty to amuse you tonight. There will be parades and pipers and dancers. *(STELLA hangs her head.)* You'll wait here for me. And if some devil comes here to take his turn while I'm gone, welcome him as you would welcome me.

STELLA *(smiling)*: Oh! Yes, gladly.

BRUNO *(frowning)*: Liar!

STELLA: I'll welcome him, truly I will.

BRUNO *(drily)*: Untruly! Untruly! If that's possible!

STELLA *(with valiant tenderness)*: Oh! Bruno, be content, your happiness is dearer to me than anything in the world. I'll tear out the pain that gnaws at you, I'll tear it out by the roots, so it will never grow again. If I've been too lazy for you, I'll be passionate from now on!

BRUNO *(stunned)*: You're trying to win me over... *(Quickly.)* Silence!

(The NURSE enters.)

It suits me to believe you now. But watch out, I can unmask you... No, don't kiss me, I'm too full of bitterness. Good night!

STELLA: Yes, good night, my love!

NURSE: Don't worry, child, be on your way without fear. I'll watch over our pet.

BRUNO: Come on, Estrugo.

(They go.)

STELLA *(at the door)*: Look, Nurse, it's almost dark. The trees in the square will be all lit up. They have woven wreaths and set lights in the branches.

Why can't I go with Bruno?

NURSE: Because he has things on his mind. All this turmoil... He needs to be alone.

STELLA: But Estrugo is going with him.

NURSE: Estrugo doesn't talk much. Oh no, he follows him like a shadow. Bruno hardly knows he's there.

(They come back in.)

STELLA *(suddenly anxious)*: Nurse, I do love Bruno, don't I?

NURSE *(stupefied)*: How could you not love Bruno? Look how he torments himself!

(Silence. STELLA sits down, weeping uncontrollably, gripped by exuberant terror and despair, as though waking up to reality.)

STELLA *(almost shouting)*: Nurse, Nurse, I'm damned! I'll go straight to hell! The devil will throw me naked onto the fire!

NURSE *(troubled)*: Darling child, what are you saying?

STELLA: I've stopped loving Bruno. I can feel it. I've stopped loving him, I'm damned, I'm an unfaithful wife!

NURSE: Now, now. Why go on like that?

STELLA: I've been unfaithful! I couldn't keep my soul free from their schemes. I thought it was best to obey without complaining. I wanted to be good, and now I've stopped loving Bruno, and I'm damned.

(She sobs.)

NURSE: Is that your fault, poor thing? Me, I can't answer for you. It's too long since I was a girl.... But maybe you're being too hard on yourself....

STELLA: I'm all alone, abandoned!...

NURSE: Well, what about me? Do I count for nothing? I'll never leave you! And if you don't want Bruno any more, well then, we'll pick someone new.

STELLA *(shaking her head forcefully)*: No! No! No! Enough!

NURSE *(laughing)*: Look at her now! Another man to take care of you. I only want what's best for you... When you were little and you were upset, I fed you warm milk from my overflowing breast, sweetened by tenderness...

STELLA *(won over, she smiles)*: Yes, yes, tell me stories. I need them to lull me to sleep... I'm weak from all their savagery. And I'm stupid, I cry, I laugh...

NURSE: ...another man, a tender man... No? All my Stella has to do is choose...

STELLA *(laughing)*: Choose? You're so naïve, you dear witch. If I was only looking for pleasure, I could pick up enough men to fill my apron. But love—how do I find that?

NURSE: My grieving child, go to sleep now. Go to sleep alone in your big bed.

STELLA *(gets up, suddenly very happy)*: Yes! All alone! Nothing could make me happier!

(The NURSE takes her to the bottom of the staircase.)

NURSE: Can you hear? The carnival is starting... You'll be able to see the parade of chinese lanterns from up there. And the carnival in the distance. (Ah! This will all come to a bad end...) Good night, my precious, fragile, wonderful girl.

STELLA *(kissing her)*: Good night, dear nurse.

(She goes up the stairs.)

NURSE: Take a bite of apple and you'll have sweet dreams. And if you don't love Bruno any more, so much the better—we'll find someone else.

STELLA *(at the top of the stairs)*: I shouldn't have confessed; now I believe I'm guilty. It will take a terrible punishment to absolve me.

NURSE *(heading for the kitchen)*: Sure! We're young, you'll get one. As for me, I clean the kitchen, I close the doors and windows, and I draw the covers up over my ears so I can't hear all the hullabaloo... Good night.

(She goes out.)

(It's night, and the moon is out.)

(The music outside has come closer. The moment STELLA reaches the landing, two MASKED MEN in costume, one of them carrying a small ladder, stop in front of the house, followed by four GUITARISTS. They are visible through the open window.)

(There are also two TORCH-BEARERS.)

(They serenade STELLA, who is leaning out the first-floor window.)

BRUNO *(outside, in falsetto):*
Now as evening darkens
the feverish willow
at the meadow's rim
seizes the slender moon
in its many arms!
You will lose her, lose her!

STELLA *(at the window)*: Who's there?

(The man carrying the ladder comes to sit on the windowsill, he takes off his black mask to breathe: ESTRUGO.)

BRUNO:
The frogs' golden eyes
glisten like constellations
at the edge of the pale ponds
and with harsh notes they rejoice
in their endless love-making.

STELLA *(amused)*: Ha! What a voice!… Are you afraid I'll recognize you?

BRUNO:
Let's do as they do, now all are asleep
and only naked love remains.

STELLA: I can't see you. At least tilt your face towards the moon. Oh! Dear God! You have hair like Bruno's, when Bruno had hair!

BRUNO:
I saw your husband walking away
bent and broken, bearing the weight of the universe
and casting before him
the shadow of his colossal horns!

STELLA *(reproachful)*: Oh! That's mean!

BRUNO: We'll deck the horns with flowers, deck them with flowers!

STELLA: Be quiet. And speak in a different voice.

BRUNO *(lyrical)*:
>You glow like a rose at dusk
>tinged by the sun's last beams
>—that ardor burns me still.
>Lucky the man who strips those petals away.

STELLA *(moved)*: Why are you here? Are you here for me? Did you come here just to say all those nice things? *(Sadly.)* Do you really need to go to such lengths to seduce me? Bruno doesn't try so hard; neither do the others!

BRUNO:
>Your fluttering voice unrolls
>like a banner
>from seraphic lips
>and your words upon it
>form heavenly signs.

STELLA: Is that a poem? Did you write it? Bruno used to write poetry! I'd be happy to listen, only please stop talking in that ridiculous voice.

BRUNO *(unable to change his voice)*:
>Your hands that clasp
>a silent solitude
>release a flight of gulls
>in this enchanted stillness.

STELLA *(melancholic)*: You're lying, but you lie well. I shouldn't listen to you, I don't deserve your singing my praises. I thank you, though.

BRUNO:
>Stella, my soul is rising
>with all the gentle calm
>of a lovely summer moon
>in a sky full of dreams.

(He laughs, bitterly.)

STELLA *(disappointed)*: Oh! Is it all just nonsense, for Saint-Géraud?

(Then she laughs.)

You're so funny! And I'm silly, letting myself be sweet-talked like that.

(Bruno gestures to Estrugo: Did you hear that?!)

BRUNO *(in his false voice)*:
    Lady, I love you, love you,
    you're so white in the light dusk
    that you seem to be falling like snow
    on chrysanthemums!

STELLA *(lets out a cry)*: Oh! Heavens! I saw you! You look like Bruno, when Bruno was handsome. That's the same clear gaze he lost, his mouth before it was silenced, his hand before it withered.

BRUNO:
    Stella, our hearts are one
    and I feel the beating of wings—
    I want to pluck your heart
    bring it down like a bird's nest—
    I'll climb the ladder!

(He leans the ladder against the house. The concert is still going on.)

STELLA *(agitated, rapidly)*: No, no, I don't want you to! I'll knock you down! You can't come in! If you love me as you say, stay down there. You scare me!

BRUNO *(climbing the steps very slowly)*:
    Your lips are dark now
    like bleeding blackberries
    and in the darkness I will taste
    their murderous juice.

STELLA *(delirious)*: Take pity on my weakness! I'm so unhappy tonight.

BRUNO:

> Like moonstones, your eyes
> —let death come now!—
> a curse upon me
> or a blessing!

(He reaches the window.)

STELLA *(out of breath)*: Yes, maybe I love you, I love you... (That voice hurts my ears.) I'll love you if you'll go away! Don't fall, it's high. Why did you climb that ladder, the door was open! Oh! I felt so abandoned! And now! Go away!

(BRUNO enters the house.)

(Now he lowers his voice.)

BRUNO *(lugubriously)*: Your hands are freezing, you're shaking. Let me warm you against me!

STELLA *(stuttering)*: I'm so frightened! Take off your mask!

BRUNO: Can you feel my heart beating? I love you. Do you love me?

STELLA: I'm all alone... Go away, you can come back tomorrow...

BRUNO: These hours are precious... This night is unique!

STELLA: Your voice frightens me... Don't kiss me! Not so hard!

(She lets out a plaintive cry.)

Oh! Why are you so awful, and so tender?

BRUNO: Come!... Come!

(He tries to drag her into the bedroom.)

STELLA *(struggling and begging)*: Oh! No, you're good... Not like this, not with you, you who love me! It's awful!... I've already lost all my hope... Don't force me, not tonight. I need tenderness, I need love... I'll love you, but take pity.

BRUNO *(drags her, keeping his great indignation in check)*: From you, I'm expecting everything. You can't refuse me... not me, not me!

STELLA: Let me give myself little by little. Let me deserve you, win me over.

BRUNO: How can you refuse me, me!

STELLA *(being dragged)*: Please drop that dismal tone of voice! I'm going mad!

(They go into the bedroom.)

(Just as they shut the door, the WOMEN of the village, lead by CORNELIA and FLORENCE, creep into the house. Outside, the music keeps playing, monotonous, hypnotic.)

CORNELIA: There's someone up there who belongs to us. Grab your sticks and hit hard.

(They prepare to climb the stairs when the bedroom door bursts open. BRUNO, still masked, rushes down the stairs shouting.)

BRUNO: With me! With me! Estrugo! With me myself, if I had wanted her to. Estrugo! I am a cuckold in every possible way!

CORNELIA *(and her companions, greeting him at the bottom of the stairs with their sticks)*: All together, now! One, two! One, two! The way we beat the chaff from the wheat. Good for nothing! Scumbag! Scoundrel! Dog!

BRUNO: Madwomen! Furies! Fiends! Stop, it's me! It's me!

(He tears off his mask.)

(The crowd is shocked, then bursts out laughing.)

(ESTRUGO enters, followed by the four GUITARISTS and the two TORCH-BEARERS who go to stand upstage. There the MUSICIANS continue to play their guitars.)

(STELLA appears at the top of the stairs and comes down, exhausted.)

STELLA: Bruno, Bruno, forgive me!

THE WOMEN *(in front of BRUNO, convulsed with joy)*: Ha! What a story! Everyone gets what they deserve!

CORNELIA: Here! Grab the slut!

CLAMOR: To the river! To the river!

BRUNO *(carried away)*: Yes, to the river, sew her up in a sack! Parade her naked through the streets on the back of a donkey! With me, Estrugo, with me! Skin the she-goat alive!

CLAMOR: Behind the mill—to the millstream where the water's deepest! To the water!

(They drag STELLA with them.)

BRUNO: Give the cheat a good soaking!

STELLA: I only cheated with you, my love!

BRUNO *(clapping his hands together)*: Exactly.

NURSE *(appears in her nightcap)*: Oh! Dear! What's all this? Stella, Stella, my kitten, where are they taking you?

BRUNO: Your kitten doesn't like water! We'll freshen her up, behind the mill.

CLAMOR: Hey! Hey! To the river!

(STELLA is lifted up and carried away.)

NURSE *(trying to follow)*: Barbarians! Savages! Cannibals!

BRUNO *(holding her back)*: Back to bed with you, bawd! Go on, get her out of here. Bravo, ladies!

NURSE *(furious)*: Oh! Dreadful boy! I take back my love, do you hear?... I detest you, I hate you, do you hear me?

And I'm going, I'm going to get her back. And I'll dig out your eyes if you try to stop me, you devil!

(She goes out and shouts.)

Stella! Stella!

(BRUNO and ESTRUGO are alone with the serenaders.)

BRUNO: Well? Now are you convinced of her worthlessness? Try to defend her now! (May her blood run cold!) Now I can't doubt any more. Oh, I'll heal, yes, I'll heal...

(He grimaces in pain.)

The ducts voiding my liver are blocked. Still, it was better to know, to take sides. Which side? Should I kill her, cast her out, forgive her?

(He suddenly gives a start.)

What? What did you say? How's that? What is it? You think that? Is that what you're saying? You think so?

She could have seen through my disguise? She was toying with me? You're sure? She saw through my subterfuge? She knew it was Bruno? You swear it?

(He moans.)

Oh! The twisted girl, the false girl, the venemous snake!

(In anguish.) But then, Estrugo, I've made no progress? I'm back to the beginning? She gave me quite a show! And the other one, the other one still exists! Ah! I have to go on looking!

(With determination.)

I give up. I know my duty. From now on, she can sleep in the fields, in the forest, in prison, I don't care where! My door is shut to her until she reveals her accomplice. If she shows up here, I'll wring her neck like a chicken.

(He takes his gun down and goes up the stairs.)

(Outside, we hear a clamor in the distance.)

(STELLA enters, wrapped in the HERDSMAN's tattered cloak, followed by the NURSE. STELLA seems very happy.)

BRUNO *(on the stairs)*: You hear that, you twisted soul! Estrugo has opened my eyes! You knew it was me! It was one of your better tricks. But don't think you've won — the person you're trying to save won't escape.

Don't look at me, Medusa!

My door is shut! My door is shut! You'll sleep under the stars, out in the cold, in wind and rain, until you confess your sin! *Ipso dixit.*

(He disappears.)

(The four MUSICIANS play on.)

(ESTRUGO sits on the window sill.)

NURSE *(with tender solicitude)*: You're not cold?

STELLA *(smiling)*: No.

NURSE: You'll sleep in my room, like when you were little!

STELLA: Yes.

NURSE: Don't be afraid, they won't come back.

STELLA: I'm not afraid.

NURSE: The herdsman can hold them back; he'll stop them. He's got big fists.

(She laughs softly.)

To think I almost killed him once! He's the one who wrapped you in his cloak. Poor dear, you were totally naked. If he hadn't saved you, they'd have paraded you through the streets on a the back of a donkey. Now, don't be ashamed. You were more graceful in your misery than all those furies in their triumph. It was pure jealousy. That Herdsman shook them up all right.

(She laughs and adds in a lower voice:)

And tomorrow we'll find you a new lover, a real one, forever and ever.

STELLA *(laughs)*: Oh! No, that's all done with.

NURSE: What? You're not planning to stay? With that torturer?

STELLA: I am.

(She laughs again, lightly.)

Hush! A moment ago, I suffered more than I thought humanly possible. Nana, it was the punishment I was hoping for. I submitted with humility and patience. And now I've paid for my fault, I'm cleansed of my sins. My soul is as white as a swan.

I'll stay here as I should. I am Bruno's wife.

When he came before, with his music and his mask, even with that dreadful voice he put on, he won back my soul. How can I explain it...? It must be that I still love him.

I'm happy, Nana. My soul is lily-white!

But... Since I can't cure Bruno, even by sacrificing my salvation, I'll stop trying. I'll punish the first fool who comes to me with his smug smile. It's my turn now.

Dear nurse, go get our room ready!

NURSE *(sighing)*: Yes... Yes... I don't understand a thing... I'm too old...

(She goes.)

(Enter the HERDSMAN confidently.)

HERDSMAN *(smiling; calm and strong)*: All done: some of those people won't forget me any time soon. Stella, now that your eyes are open, come with me.

STELLA *(decisively)*: No!

HERDSMAN *(confidently)*: Yes. You can't stay with Bruno after all that.

STELLA: I can.

HERDSMAN (*still confident*): No. You'll come live with me in my cabin, with all the animals around us. We can share my bed. It's not very big. I'll keep you.

STELLA: No, no and no! Go away. I thank you very much.

HERDSMAN (*suddenly furious*): Give me back my cloak!

STELLA (*backing away*): I can't. I'm naked underneath.

HERDSMAN (*holding his hand out*): Too bad.

STELLA (*terrified*): Oh! No!

HERDSMAN (*advancing*): I'm not the only one who's seen you without your feathers.

STELLA (*tries to escape at right*): Wait a minute, I'll put on a dress, then I'll give it back.

HERDSMAN (*blocking her path*): No. I didn't make you wait, did I?

STELLA (*begging*): At least let me call my nurse.

HERDSMAN (*stubborn*): Come with me!

STELLA (*violently*): No, no, no! Beast!

HERDSMAN (*grabs her brusquely*): Well then, I'll take my turn, too.

STELLA (*cries out, very loudly*): No! I don't want to! Never!

(*At the sound of her cries, BRUNO appears above, looks, listens.*)

HERDSMAN (*furious*): You're coming whether you want to or not, dead or alive.

STELLA (*struggling against him*): No! No! Animal!

(*She has broken free and slaps the boy hard across the face.*)

BRUNO (*yells*): She's hitting him! She hit me! It's him, it must be him!

(*He points his gun at the HERDSMAN.*)

(*STELLA, jumping at the man and madly kissing him on the mouth.*)

STELLA (*passionately*): Yes, yes, I love you! Take me away! You'll keep me!

HERDSMAN (*simply*): Come.

STELLA *(on the doorstep)*: Wait. First promise me—swear—that I can be faithful to you.

(She goes.)

(BRUNO sits down on the stair and laughs.)

BRUNO: Oh, no, no, I'm not that stupid... It's just another one of her tricks! You won't fool me this time!

CURTAIN

This translation of *The Magnificent Cuckold*
was printed in Garamond.
The edition consists of 100 numbered copies
of which six are lettered from A to F.

This is copy **3**.

The illustration on the end papers is by Lyobov Popova.
It was made for the 1923 production by Vsevolod Meyerhold.